NEW DIRECTIONS FOR TEACHING AND LEARNING

Marilla D. Svinicki, *University of Texas, Austin*
EDITOR-IN-CHIEF

R. Eugene Rice, *American Associa*
CONSULTING EDITOR

Evaluating Teaching in Higher Education: A Vision for the Future

Katherine E. Ryan
University of Illinois at Urbana-Champaign

EDITOR

Number 83, Fall 2000

JOSSEY-BASS
San Francisco

EVALUATING TEACHING IN HIGHER EDUCATION: A VISION FOR THE FUTURE
Katherine E. Ryan (ed.)
New Directions for Teaching and Learning, no. 83
Marilla D. Svinicki, Editor-in-Chief
R. Eugene Rice, Consulting Editor

Microfilm copies of issues and articles are available in 16mm and 35mm, as well as microfiche in 105mm, through University Microfilms Inc., 300 North Zeeb Road, Ann Arbor, Michigan 48106-1346.

ISSN 0271-0633   ISBN 0-7879-5448-9

NEW DIRECTIONS FOR TEACHING AND LEARNING is part of The Jossey-Bass Higher and Adult Education Series and is published quarterly by Jossey-Bass Inc., 350 Sansome Street, San Francisco, California 94104-1342. Periodicals postage paid at San Francisco, California, and at additional mailing offices. Postmaster: Send address changes to New Directions for Teaching and Learning, Jossey-Bass Inc., 350 Sansome Street, San Francisco, California 94104-1342.

New Directions for Teaching and Learning is indexed in College Student Personnel Abstracts, Contents Pages in Education, and Current Index to Journals in Education (ERIC).

SUBSCRIPTIONS cost $58.00 for individuals and $104.00 for institutions, agencies, and libraries. Prices subject to change.

EDITORIAL CORRESPONDENCE should be sent to the editor-in-chief, Marilla D. Svinicki, The Center for Teaching Effectiveness, University of Texas at Austin, Main Building 2200, Austin, TX 78712-1111.

Cover photograph by Richard Blair/Color & Light © 1990.

www.josseybass.com

Contents

FROM THE SERIES EDITORS

About This Publication. Since 1980, *New Directions for Teaching and Learning* (NDTL) has brought a unique blend of theory, research, and practice to leaders in postsecondary education. NDTL sourcebooks strive not only for solid substance but also for timeliness, compactness, and accessibility.

The series has four goals: to inform readers about current and future directions in teaching and learning in postsecondary education, to illuminate the context that shapes these new directions, to illustrate these new directions through examples from real settings, and to propose ways in which these new directions can be incorporated into still other settings.

This publication reflects our view that teaching deserves respect as a high form of scholarship. We believe that significant scholarship is conducted not only by researchers who report results of empirical investigations but also by practitioners who share disciplined reflections about teaching. Contributors to NDTL approach questions of teaching and learning as seriously as they approach substantive questions in their own disciplines, and they deal not only with pedagogical issues but also with the intellectual and social context in which these issues arise. Authors deal on the one hand with theory and research and on the other with practice, and they translate from research and theory to practice and back again.

About This Volume. This volume focuses on important developments in the area of evaluating teaching in higher education. Moving away from the old arguments about whether teaching should or can be evaluated, the authors focus more on alternatives to the traditional views of evaluation and the philosophies behind them. They urge us to look beyond what we do now to what we might do tomorrow.

MARILLA D. SVINICKI, editor-in-chief, is director of the Center for Teaching Effectiveness at the University of Texas, Austin.

R. EUGENE RICE, consulting editor, is director, Forum on Faculty Roles and Rewards, AAHE.

Editor's Notes

What should the evaluation of teaching in higher education look like as the new century unfolds? A diverse group of scholars and scholar practitioners collectively propose a vision in the chapters in this volume of *New Directions for Teaching and Learning*. Their vision is organized around three recurring themes they identify as critical in considering evaluation in the new century: how to evaluate teaching in higher education, how to address the multiple purposes involved in the evaluation of teaching, and who should decide how to evaluate college teaching. More specifically, each scholar or scholar practitioner addresses the lack of consensus on how to evaluate teaching. They propose possible solutions to the fundamental complexities inherent in addressing college teaching evaluation from a personnel perspective as well as a developmental perspective, while simultaneously dealing with institutional goals. Finally, the notion of who should decide how to evaluate teaching and how to evaluate teaching is broadened substantially in their discussions. Given the recent emphasis on improving undergraduate teaching and the fundamental shifts in the notion of what constitutes faculty work, these tensions need to be addressed.

Each chapter examines the evaluation of teaching in higher education from a different perspective, with each perspective portraying a distinct turn on the themes, and identifies the issues facing us now. Chapters One through Four sketch the broad landscape of the evaluation of teaching. Speaking from a critical perspective in Chapter One, Robert Menges discusses some shortcomings in the evaluation of teaching and suggests they are quite diverse, including preoccupation with the empirical over the theoretical and a preference for quantitative rather than qualitative approaches. On the other hand, John Ory, in Chapter Two, takes the positive position, highlighting achievements in the evaluation of teaching over the past thirty years. Stressing the evolution of teaching evaluation, he notes that sources of evidence for teaching effectiveness are characterized by systematic procedures and strong methods. In Chapter Three, Larry Braskamp takes up the future of evaluation. Offering an extensive discussion of the implications for the future of higher education on the evaluation of teaching, he emphasizes the importance of experimentation and examination of the dual roles of teaching and learning in charting the course of teaching evaluation. Randall Bass, in Chapter Four, offers a comprehensive analysis of how technology alters the meaning of teaching and learning and the implications of these changes for the evaluation of teaching. From the intersection of technology, evaluation, and the visibility of teaching and learning, he proposes three key issues for consideration.

The authors of Chapters Five through Eight present snapshots of a collective vision of the evaluation of teaching in higher education. In Chapter Five, emphasizing the evaluation as situational, Robert Stake and Edith Cisneros-Cohernour propose that the evaluation of teaching should reach beyond and expand the notion of the lone instructor in a single classroom. The extension provides an illustration of how to evaluate teaching using a community of practice approach that provides feedback through collective peer evaluations. Daniel Bernstein, Jessica Jonson, and Karen Smith, in Chapter Six, report on the impact of the implementation of peer review of teaching from a study that Bernstein conducted with thirty faculty members. The peer review included written interactions with disciplinary colleagues on the intellectual substance of the course, classroom practice, and student learning. Changes in a wide range of key measures were examined in relationship to the nature and intensity of the peer review process. Proposing a teaching portfolio as a vehicle for the evaluation of teaching in Chapter Seven, John Centra describes how the colleagues of an instructor can assess instructional quality through portfolios and other self-reported sources of information on teaching. In Chapter Eight, Michael Theall and Jennifer Franklin provide an extensive critical analysis of student ratings of instruction, the most common and widely used form of evaluation. Emphasizing the changing context of instruction, they argue that student ratings forms tend to be mismatched with the newer instructional approaches such as active and cooperative learning. They offer suggestions on how to make student ratings more responsive.

In the closing chapter, Trav Johnson and Katherine Ryan use common themes from the issue chapters as a framework for discussing the implication of the themes for evaluation practice. They present a multifaceted approach as a first effort at translating the collective vision proposed here for evaluating teaching in higher education.

Katherine E. Ryan
Editor

KATHERINE E. RYAN is associate professor of educational psychology at the University of Illinois at Urbana-Champaign.

A Tribute to Robert Menges

Lawrence A. Braskamp

This volume of the *New Directions for Teaching and Learning* is dedicated to the late Robert Menges, a former editor of this series and a contributor to this volume. It is fitting to honor Bob for his leadership and scholarship and, of course, his influence on so many of us who knew him personally and those who know him through his writings and the work of his students. We are privileged in many ways to read the latest and last thinking of a scholar who had a wide range of intellectual interests in the fields of learning and development in higher education. As you will read, he did not try to simplify the complexity of the issues posed in his research—in this case, the evaluation of teaching. He had a grasp on the relevant theories and on practice that we admired. He was unusual in his ability to listen and learn from feedback. When you read the chapter in this volume, remember that Bob died just three days before he was to deliver a paper (which is the unedited chapter) and that most likely he would have made some changes given his ability to learn from his colleagues.

Bob presented his ideas with considerable and careful thought and deliberation. He loved to share, edit and give feedback to others as well. But perhaps what we can best learn from this chapter and from his other writings and his work as a professor is his intense interest, care, and pride in his students. As a colleague in a nearby university, we often shared our thoughts, interests, and concerns abut higher education. To him, students always took first place. He was concerned that our emphasis on research could devalue the student as a person. He worked hard at Northwestern University and other places where he consulted to stress the importance of being a teacher and mentor in the life of the scholar. Scholars both teach and learn, as do students. He had the right balance, in my view. His scholarship as illustrated in the chapter in this volume nicely reflects the life of a scholar who was able to demonstrate a blend of wisdom, kindness, and a love of people. For this we are grateful.

LAWRENCE A. BRASKAMP is chief academic officer of Loyola University Chicago.

1

Although much has been learned from research on teaching in higher education, much still remains unknown, and most remains unused by practitioners themselves.

Shortcomings of Research on Evaluating and Improving Teaching in Higher Education

Robert Menges

My text for this meditative essay on the state of educational research is taken from the Gospel According to Ms. Mentor, as recorded by Emily Toth in the wonderful book entitled *Ms. Mentor's Impeccable Advice for Women in Academia.*[1] In answer to a question about getting good student evaluations, Ms. Mentor makes the following observations:

> Realists do, of course, know the single thing that does the most to improve a teacher's evaluations: giving high grades. Occasionally a researcher in the *Chronicle of Higher Education* will claim there is no correlation between students' grades and their evaluations of their teachers. Perhaps the researchers are not deliberate liars, says Ms. Mentor, but they are surely wrong [Toth, 1997, p. 95].

Ms. Mentor here gives voice to some widely shared perceptions about student evaluations of teaching, despite their being one of the most researched areas in higher education. We will return to Ms. Mentor later and consider why she and so many others continue to think this way, but for now, our topic is much broader than student evaluations of teaching. It is the state of research on teaching in higher education as a whole.

Note: This chapter was edited posthumously by Marilla D. Svinicki, University of Texas at Austin.

New Directions for Teaching and Learning, no. 83, Fall 2000   © Jossey-Bass, a Wiley company

I speak from the experience of reviewing this research for a chapter in the *Handbook of Research on Teaching* (Menges and Austin, forthcoming). The amount of research about teaching in higher education and the variety of places in which it appears have expanded considerably since the last edition of the *Handbook* was published in 1986. I was impressed with the extent and potential value of what is known in many areas. For example, we know a great deal about small group learning, about students' contributions to evaluating teaching, and about the academic reward structure as it relates to teaching. On the other hand, there is much more information than wisdom in this literature. Even so, the impact that all this research has had on practice is far less than is warranted.

In the Menges and Austin *Handbook* chapter, we identified four significant bodies of research about teaching in higher education: (1) about faculty as teachers, (2) about students as learners, (3) about the content being taught and learned, and (4) about the environments in which teaching and learning occur, including research on various methods of instruction. We depicted these areas and their relationships as shown in Figure 1.1, expecting that studies in the areas of overlap are likely to yield the most important findings and have the greatest impact. This would be true especially in the central area, where investigators would simultaneously consider teachers, learners, content, and method—and the relationships among those elements. Had we been able to count the number of studies that fell into each area and draw Figure 1.1 to scale, the size of that central area would be considerably smaller.

Shortcomings of Research in Higher Education

Let me illustrate four areas where educational research is substantial yet much less useful than it could and should be. For each area, I include an

Figure 1.1. Framework for Research About Teaching in Higher Education

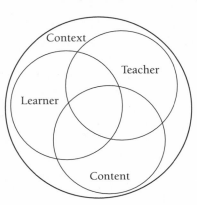

important question that I believe we should be able to answer but for which educational research is inadequate.

Area 1: Faculty Behaviors and Intentions. We know a good deal about what faculty do as teachers: how they spend their time, what their goals for students are, what instructional methods they use, how method selections are influenced by other variables (such as one's discipline), and the extent to which method choices are constant or variable over time. We know much less about why faculty teach the way they do. How do they derive their personal theories of teaching and learning? Under what conditions do they act or fail to act according to their personal theories? How do they compare their actual attainments with their intentions, and what are the consequences when they do? And, most important for the field of educational research, what roles in this process, if any, are played by research findings and formal theories?

If we knew more about why faculty teach as they do, we would be able to respond to the following significant and practical question:

> Why do faculty fail to use demonstrably effective teaching methods and other data-based information about teaching, and how can that situation be changed?

Area 2: Technology-Mediated Instruction. Interactive, multimedia instructional technologies hold great promise, which reviews of research are beginning to document. But much remains to be learned. For example, are students who have grown up in the information age different as learners in postsecondary education from their predecessors? Do they process information differently? Are they more likely to welcome discovery and participative approaches to learning? Are they able to function in virtual worlds as effectively as in the real world?

Even more critical, we know little about what types of learning are best supported by electronic technologies. What types of learning are best gained through peer interactions or by students working independently? What types are best gained through direct faculty-student interaction? Much new research is required if we are to understand, for example, the distinctive characteristics of student-faculty instructional interactions compared with technologically mediated instruction.

This topic has a vitally important question, which we cannot now answer:

> What are the essential contributions (to student learning, satisfaction, and development) of face-to-face instructional interactions between teachers and students that cannot be provided as effectively by technology?

Area 3: Effective Evaluative Decisions. Research tells a great deal about gathering information that is potentially useful for decisions about assessing and improving teaching and learning. Little is known, however, about how decisions using that information are made. For example, how do students decide what to say when evaluating their courses and their teachers? How do administrators and colleagues use evaluation information when assessing faculty performance? How do teachers themselves use evaluation information in planning, implementing, and appraising their own teaching? A great many individuals in the assessment area would assert that no matter how valid and reliable the instrument is, consumers can and do misuse the results from it. Is there a way to overcome that difficulty, through better instrumentation or better training of the consumers?

Research in this area would permit us to respond, for example, to the following urgent question:

> How does information from student evaluation of teaching affect retention, tenure, and promotion deliberations and decisions?

Area 4: Context-Specific Research. My final choice of area where research has serious shortcomings concerns context-specific research. Research we have reviewed from the past decade is predominantly quantitative in method, conducted largely by persons trained in positivist traditions of psychology and sociology, seek generalizations while controlling for variation. Recent work has begun to recognize the importance of context-specific investigations, including personal, organizational, and political contexts, as well as the perspectives of the participants in teaching and learning. This requires moving beyond surveys (or any other single method) and drawing on less traditional and more varied sources of data.

For this topic, the question is one that we must apply to our own investigations:

> Does our research include each of the following: data about the participants (both internal and external perspectives); information about content being taught and learned; and information about personal, organization, and political contexts in which teaching and learning is occurring?

Constructive Redirections for Future Research

Enough about shortcomings. Let me now try to be more constructive. I want to develop briefly two directions for the field that I think could move us toward answers for important questions like those I have raised.

Research Methods. The first direction relates to the topic of research methods themselves and to the central area of Figure 1.1. In that area of overlap, a researcher is seeking access to the activities of teaching and learning (externally, through reports of observers and analysis of recordings), to the actors (internally, through reports from teachers and learners about their thoughts, feelings, and cognitions), and to the content (teacher materials and performance measures from learners), along with information about contextual features that impinge on these events. Broadening the way we research questions in this area could provide much more information than we usually get.

For example, suppose that we are researching classroom explanations of course content. Investigators might study the explanations of core concepts that are given by teachers in several disciplines in both lecture and small group settings, and compare them with explanations given by students in peer tutoring or reciprocal teaching settings. Data might include observations of verbal and nonverbal interactions, reflections by teachers and learners on what transpired during those interactions (as well as before and after the interactions), and indicators of what learners have come to understand about the concepts. All of these options would yield much richer data than is typical in higher education research.

These studies are feasible and would enrich theory and understanding. What is their potential for advancing practice? That is our next direction.

Influencing Practice. My second direction for the field has to do with the topic of influencing practice. This brings us back to Ms. Mentor, her views about research on student evaluations of teaching, and her advice about what to do to get high evaluations. (She advises, by the way, that in addition to giving high grades, the teacher help students to feel positively disposed toward the teacher before evaluation forms are distributed and that evaluation forms be revised to reflect women's teaching styles better.)

My concern is how we go about studying teachers' practices in order to understand and eventually change them. What is needed is a deeper understanding of practitioners and the practices they follow. This includes examining their theories-in-action and how and why theories-in-action differ from espoused theories. In short, we need what Schön (1995) has called an epistemology of practice.

In thinking about practices and how to understand them, I welcome Robinson's (1998) recent discussion in the *Educational Researcher* about the research-practice gap. In her view, that gap persists partly because we do not adequately understand practice. As she puts it, "Research may be ignored, regardless of how skillfully it is communicated, because it by-passes the problem-solving processes that sustain the practices that researchers seek to alter" (p. 17). Exploring practice therefore requires us to discern the problem for which the practice serves as a solution. This includes making inferences about how participants formulate the problem, identify potential solutions, and choose among solutions.

Returning now to the example from Ms. Mentor, we see that the practice in question is that faculty attempt to inflate student ratings. Through our research, we should seek to understand what problem faculty are trying to solve when they attempt to inflate grades. For example, they might be trying to solve the problem of how to generate data that will portray them as effective teachers during tenure and promotion decisions. In trying to solve this problem, what other solutions do they consider? What criteria led them to the decision that inflating grades was the best choice? What views, if any, do students and other significant actors have of these matters? Tentative findings would then be checked with the teachers, their students, and perhaps colleagues and chairs.

By understanding how teachers think and solve their practice problems, researchers might be able to identify the kinds of data that would be useful to those problems. That in itself would encourage more practitioners to use research findings. For example, if a large number of teachers are selecting practices aimed at the problem of student motivation, they would be most interested in and receptive to research that would help them clarify what motivation is and how it operates in the classroom.

Second, if researchers understand how teachers make practice decisions, we might be able to design interventions that would have a greater probability of getting teachers to change their practice to be more in line with research findings. So, for example, if teachers make their decisions primarily on the basis of anecdotal data rather than statistical data, researchers would be well advised to gather qualitative data along with their quantitative data and to use the former as an entry to teacher interest and the latter to back up the conclusions.

Conclusion

In this chapter, I have shared four topics about which I believe research is substantial but still far short of complete. And I have suggested two ways by which we can make progress. First, our investigations should simultaneously consider all the key variables of teachers, learners, content, and method and the relationships among them. Second, in our investigation of teacher practices, some of which we will want to change, we must understand them as responses to problems for which the practice serves as a solution if we want to be successful in changing them. Research that informs either of these two areas would be most beneficial for future progress in higher education.

Note

1. Emily Toth describes her creation, Ms. Mentor, as "a crotchety spirit who never leaves her ivory tower, from which she dispenses her perfect wisdom on all things academic. Like her counterpart, Ms. Manners, Ms. Mentor is impeccably knowledgeable and self-confident, and knows much more than anyone will ever ask" (Toth, 1997, p. ix).

References

Menges, R. J., and Austin, A. E. (forthcoming). "Teaching in Higher Education." In V. Richardson (Ed.), *Handbook of Research on Teaching*. Washington, D.C.: American Educational Research Association.

Robinson, V.M.J. "Methodology and the Research-Practice Gap." *Educational Researcher,* 1998, *27,* 17–26.

Schön, D. A. "Knowing-in-Action: The New Scholarship Requires a New Epistemology." *Change,* 1995, *27*(6), 27–34.

Toth, E. *Ms. Mentor's Impeccable Advice for Women in Academia.* Philadelphia: University of Pennsylvania Press, 1997.

ROBERT MENGES was a professor of higher education at Northwestern University. He presented the contents of this chapter at a meeting of the American Educational Research Association before his death in the spring of 1998.

2

The purpose and methodology of teaching evaluation in higher education have changed significantly from the past.

Teaching Evaluation: Past, Present, and Future

John C. Ory

During the past thirty years teaching evaluation in higher education has changed significantly. The two facets that have changed the most are purpose and methodology. For years, teaching evaluation has been conducted as a response to different audiences with different needs for information. In the 1960s, teaching evaluation was conducted primarily in response to student demands for public accountability. Many campus student government organizations became actively involved in the collection of student ratings of instruction for purposes of faculty evaluation and improved course selection. In the 1970s teaching evaluation was done for more developmental reasons. Evaluation information was collected to help faculty improve and develop. During this time campus, faculty development and instructional support offices similar to my own proliferated.

In the 1980s and 1990s teaching evaluation was driven by administrative rather than faculty or student needs. The demands of budgetary deficits and retrenchment caused administrators to rely on the collection of additional evaluative information and make new uses of information already being collected on campus. In recent years several additional audiences and demands for teaching evaluation have appeared: the resurgence of national interest in the improvement of undergraduate education (Astin, 1991; Erwin, 1991), public demand for college and university accountability (Bok, 1992; Ewell, 1991), and the demand from the nation's legal system (Centra, 1993) for more and improved teaching evaluation. A fourth demand is coming from today's faculty, especially the new assistant professors. I believe the faculty, especially young professors, are now making demands on teaching evaluation to be fairer and more accurate—to be a better portrayal of the complexity of their work today (Boyer, 1990). In essence, they are saying, "Help me to improve, but help me to show what I am worth."

Regarding the demands from the nation's legal system, a weekly reading of the *Chronicle of Higher Education* reveals that decisions on faculty promotion, tenure, and merit pay are frequently being challenged in the courts. Today's administrators face the ever-present threat of litigation and must be able to support their decisions with tangible and objective evaluative information. In this regard, Ken Eble (1984) described the campuses of the 1980s (and we could easily say today's campuses) as having a "litigious academic atmosphere."

The public demand for accountability is represented by the outcomes assessment movement in today's colleges and universities (Boyer, 1987; National Institute of Education, 1984). While the primary focus of assessment has been on student achievement or outcomes, a close look at most university assessment procedures reveals that teaching evaluation is a component in virtually all of them.

In sum, teaching evaluation in higher education has had to accommodate many audiences with different purposes. I strongly believe that purpose affects methods. Consequently, changes in the audiences and purposes of teaching evaluation have caused changes in the methodology of teaching evaluation. Teaching evaluation in higher education has evolved from a primary reliance on a chair's assessment to a formal, systematic, and multiple approach, including a variety of methods like student ratings, peer reviews, peer visits, self-evaluations, document reviews, and evidence of achievement. As new purposes and audiences were added, so too were new evaluation methods or new ways of using old methods. For example, student ratings became more of a normative-quality measure for administrators than an aid for student course selection. The development of a comprehensive set of methods responded to legal considerations. The use of self-evaluations was emphasized for developmental purposes. And we now see increased interest in teaching portfolios, especially from young faculty who do not believe that existing methods do justice to their work.

Teaching evaluation in higher education is no longer what George Geis (1984) called a "shifting and ambiguous activity" or what scholars Chickering (1984) and Eble (1984) described as a "seat-of-the-pants process," wherein "casual praise from a single student or a casual impression of a public performance could pass as substantial evidence." Instead, formal, comprehensive, and systematic approaches to teaching evaluation have been developed and implemented at a growing number of colleges and universities. Institutions are collecting more information from multiple audiences and taking more care in doing so than ever before. Teaching evaluation is no longer the sole responsibility of the dean or department chair, and as a consequence, there has been a gradual diffusion of decision-making power. On many of today's campuses, committees composed of faculty and administrators are making personnel and program decisions based on systematically collected information.

The finding has also been noted by Peter Seldin when he compared a 1988 and 1998 nationwide survey results of college teaching evaluation practices. Seldin (1998) wrote: "To me, this [change in survey results from 1988 to 1998] indicates that the information-gathering process is becoming more structured and widespread, and that the colleges are making a concerted effort to reexamine and shore up their approach to evaluating teaching" (p. 4).

So what has been the impact of these changes in purpose and methods? On the positive side of the ledger is greater comprehensiveness, less attention to nonperformance characteristics, more use of data in informed discussion, more care in collecting data, and a diffusion of decision-making power. In other words, in making personnel decisions, today's faculty and administration use a wider range and quantity of pertinent data that have been more carefully collected than in the past. But some educators would argue that the departure from informal assessment and the development of formal, comprehensive systems for teaching evaluation have placed too much emphasis on supporting personnel decision making and too little emphasis on developing faculty or improving curriculum.

The fact is that the utilization of evaluation results has been limited on most campuses to aiding the decision-making process only. The linkage between evaluation results and faculty or course improvement or between campus evaluation and faculty development offices has yet to be fully explored. For example, how many campuses with student rating systems have available procedures that faculty can follow or people to contact to seek help after obtaining low ratings? Or what can faculty members do to improve their teaching when they receive a poor three-year review as an assistant professor?

To be useful, teaching evaluation has to become a feedback process. Given the aging of faculty and the public demand for better teaching, we need to consider ways of using comprehensive evaluation systems to provide faculty with feedback, or "information about their performance that includes recommendations for future improvement."

For several years my colleague Larry Braskamp and I (Braskamp and Ory, 1994) started to refer to faculty evaluation as faculty assessment when we discovered that the word *assess* is derived from the Latin word *assidere,* meaning "to sit beside." By using the word *assessment,* we wish to recapture the connotation of "to sit beside."

"Sitting beside" is a metaphor for assessment that encompasses several themes. "To sit beside" brings to mind such verbs as *to engage, to involve, to interact, to share, to trust.* It conjures up team learning, working together, discussing, reflecting, helping, building, and collaborating. It makes one think of cooperative learning, community, communication, coaching, caring, and consultation. When two people "sit beside" each other, engaged in assessing, one may very well be judging and providing feedback about the other's performance, but the style and context of the exchange are critical. "Sitting beside" implies dialogue and discourse, with one person trying to understand the other's perspective before giving value judgments.

Assessment as "sitting beside" promotes a developmental perspective. It is not a single snapshot but rather a continuous view. It facilitates development rather than classifying and ranking the faculty by some predetermined measurement such as a student rating item or number of publications. It encourages breaking away from the winner-loser mind-set, comparing one person to another. Instead the focus is on understanding the colleague's perspective and achievements, which means the focus is on real-world performance.

In our definition of assessment, we emphasize four processes.

The first process is that *assessment examines the craft of the work*. In addition to identifying the activities themselves, faculty should have an opportunity to describe the thinking behind their work (Lynton, 1992). How and why did they decide to spend more time one year helping the state transportation agency rather than working on a second research grant? Why did they choose to develop an on-line distance-learning course? By examining the craft of their work, faculty are more likely to use multiple measures and strategies, develop assessment techniques that highlight uniqueness rather than conformity and uniformity, and integrate assessment and evaluation with faculty and institutional development.

The second process is that *faculty members reflect on the quality of their work and discuss standards with colleagues and chairs or heads*. In addition to having an opportunity to discuss the thinking behind their work, faculty should also have an opportunity to comment on its quality and contribution to the institution, field of study, or society at large. They should be able to make a case for the quality and impact of their efforts. Presentations of faculty cases should also help to develop a consensual understanding of what the department and institution accepts as standards of quality. Too often these standards of quality are assumed and go years without clarification. One wonders how young faculty learn what is and is not viewed as quality work.

Third, *faculty receive feedback from others and are expected to use it to improve their work*. Assessment as "sitting beside" means faculty sitting together in a friendly, formative way discussing their work; observing a classroom or a performance; and taking notes trying to describe and understand in a nonevaluative way what the colleague is doing or administrators asking faculty about their personal goals and explaining institutional expectations.

Fourth, *colleagues assess the work of others by focusing on the value of the work while keeping in mind the institutional mission and encouraging the institution to value faculty work more highly*. In a recent meeting, a campus administrator praised the national reputation of a professor's Web site and called for similar efforts. He was quite surprised to hear from someone in the room how the professor's Web site was not going to be mentioned in the upcoming promotion review for fear of negatively affecting the decision. Campus and departmental values and priorities need to be discussed, debated, and reviewed periodically.

I recently participated on a panel discussing post-tenure reviews. It became clear to me as I listened to the other panelists how well the "sitting beside" notion of faculty evaluation fits the needs of these reviews, especially if we believe that these reviews should be more developmental than punitive. If we want to conduct post-tenure reviews to keep faculty productive, we need to understand their interests, goals, and motivations better. If we want to conduct post-tenure reviews to get faculty to do more for the institution, we need to communicate our needs and expectations. A faculty member on the panel spoke of his failure to receive feedback about his job performance for the past twenty years, or since he received tenure. As faculty age, their goals change as do their contributions. I believe that both individuals and institutions profit from post-tenure reviews that encourage administrators and faculty to sit beside one another and discuss mutual needs and rewards.

Assessment is more than counting, measuring, recording, or accounting. It promotes teaching evaluation not as a scientific endeavor, with absolute truth as its goal, but rather as a form of argument where the faculty use their data to make a case for their teaching. It incorporates the institutional context, the role of colleagues in judging and helping others, and the need to observe the actual work of the faculty. It touches on self-reflection, dialogue, and discussion. It is learning, developing, and building.

The development of comprehensive evaluation systems has improved the decision-making process on many campuses. Indeed, a broad repertoire of assessment methods is needed to capture the work of faculty. But good assessment is more than expanding methods of collecting evidence. Campuses in the future need to create a culture of assessment, where every activity is not judged and assigned a numerical value or where faculty members are not constantly ranked against their colleagues, but rather a culture that allows faculty to discuss openly with each other and their administrators their goals and accomplishments. They must be given an opportunity to show what they have done, what they are doing, and what they can do. The assessment must improve both individuals and institutions.

References

Astin, A. W. *Assessment for Excellence: The Philosophy and Practice of Assessment and Evaluation.* New York: American Council on Education, 1991.

Bok, D. "Reclaiming the Public Trust." *Change,* Jul.–Aug. 1992, pp. 12–19.

Boyer, E. L. *College: The Undergraduate Experience in America.* New York: HarperCollins, 1987.

Boyer, E. L. *Scholarship Reconsidered: Priorities of the Professoriate.* Princeton, N.J.: Carnegie Foundation for the Advancement of Teaching, 1990.

Braskamp, L. A., and Ory, J. C. *Assessing Faculty Work.* San Francisco: Jossey-Bass, 1994.

Centra, J. A. *Reflective Faculty Evaluation.* San Francisco: Jossey-Bass, 1993.

Chickering, A. W. "Faculty Evaluations: Problems and Solutions." In P. Seldin (ed.), *Changing Practices in Faculty Evaluation.* San Francisco: Jossey-Bass, 1984.

Eble, K. E. "New Directions in Faculty Evaluation." In P. Seldin (ed.), *Changing Practices in Faculty Evaluation.* San Francisco: Jossey-Bass, 1984.

Erwin, T. D. *Assessing Student Learning and Development.* San Francisco: Jossey-Bass, 1991.

Ewell, P. T. "Assessment and Public Accountability: Back to the Future." *Change,* Nov.–Dec. 1991, pp. 12–17.

Geis, G. L. "The Context of Evaluation." In P. Seldin (ed.) *Changing Practices in Faculty Evaluation.* San Francisco: Jossey-Bass, 1984.

Lynton, E. A. "Scholarship Recognized." Report to the Carnegie Foundation for the Advancement of Teaching, Boston, September 1992.

National Institute of Education. *Involvement in Learning: Realizing the Potential of American Higher Education.* Washington, D.C.: U.S. Department of Education, 1984.

Seldin, P. *AAHE Bulletin,* Mar. 1998.

JOHN C. ORY is director of the Office of Instructional Resources at the University of Illinois at Urbana-Champaign.

3

Assessing faculty as teachers requires creatively integrating four elements.

Toward a More Holistic Approach to Assessing Faculty as Teachers

Lawrence A. Braskamp

Our strategies for the evaluation and assessment of faculty as teachers depend on our view of the role of faculty in higher education and in the larger community. (I use *evaluation* and *assessment* interchangeably in this chapter. See note 1 at the end of the chapter for a definition.)

I begin by highlighting two images of the work of faculty, as well as the presumptions and implications of these images. These two images are portrayed in the extreme at times, to make their distinctions as clear as possible. Yet both converge around the centrality of community in teaching and learning, and thus they are more complementary than I tend to present them; I do so to make their distinctions as clear as possible. Then I conclude the first part of the chapter by presenting my perspective on the assessment of teaching by answering four questions: Why do we assess? What are the standards and criteria of quality and effectiveness? What should we assess? and How can we assess?

As I began to reflect on my ideas and have conversations with others about the value of the four elements in assessment, I wondered if faculty would accept, much less reinforce, the centrality of the teacher—his or her identity, scholarship, and character—in assessing the contributions of a faculty member. As a result, I decided to meet with faculty at Loyola University Chicago to discuss some answers to these questions: How would faculty react to my ideas about the elements in the evaluation of faculty? What

---

Note: This chapter is a revision of papers presented at the annual meetings of the American Educational Research Association, April 1998, San Diego, California, and April 1999, Montreal.

issues, concerns, and priorities would they emphasize in their dialogue about teaching, particular? I conclude with my perspective of the future of the assessment of higher education faculty, based on my dialogues with the Loyola faculty and feedback from others about the elements of assessing teaching. (For a further and more personal account of the context of my writing this chapter, first as a professor at the University of Illinois Chicago, and then as the chief academic officer at Loyola University Chicago, see note 2 at the end of the chapter.)

Elements of Assessing Teaching

In my thinking about the assessment of teaching, I have concluded that some fundamental elements must be included in assessments. I have selected four, as well as one integrating and integrative element.

Two Images. I have developed two images to describe the role of faculty as teachers in higher education. Four elements—the teacher and teaching, the learner (student) and learning—are the building blocks. One image begins with student learning and the fundamental belief that colleges are to produce learning, not just to provide instruction. Barr and Tagg, in a widely read article in *Change,* argue, "We now see that our mission is not instruction but rather that of producing *learning* with every student by *whatever* means work best" (1995, p. 13). The focus is on locating the most cost-effective methods and tools for improving student learning. What are the presumptions and implications of this image?

First, the complexity of student learning is acknowledged. The research on the teaching–learning process has focused on learning rather than teaching in the past two decades, and for good reason. Cognitive psychologists have advanced our understanding of how humans learn, and we know it is more than simple stimulus-reflex connections (Ewell, 1997; McKeachie, 1997; Shulman, 1999). There is a clear recognition that students differ. Thus, student learning styles, ethnic backgrounds, prior knowledge, and skill levels are given credence. For example, adults prefer problem-centered learning situations and prefer faculty to be fellow facilitators rather than distant experts. This image makes sense as we begin to construct the cyber-campus, capitalizing on the power of distance education and the unique learning situations made possible by instructional technology. Teaching and learning can occur virtually anytime and anywhere. Some have even proposed that we think in terms of learning units—like chucks of a material object—to be produced and then measured.

Second, faculty are regarded as one factor, albeit a critical one, in producing learning. They often are viewed as partners with the students rather than masters or special learners, except that they are employees of an institution with responsibility for producing learning. Faculty work as coaches, mentors, and learners. The predominant image of the teacher is "the guide on the side and not the sage on stage." Moreover, faculty have no inherent privilege or advantage for producing learning; the computer, in fact, may be a more effective and efficient tool. In this regard Barr and Tagg state, "In the Learning Paradigm, learning environments and activities are learner-centered and learner-controlled. They may even be 'teacherless.' While teachers will have designed the learning experiences and environments students use—often through teamwork with each other and other staff—they need not be present for or participate in every structured learning activity" (1995, pp. 21–22).

The other image of the faculty in higher education is almost the opposite: the teacher as a person in the teaching-learning process is highlighted. Parker Palmer is perhaps the most articulate advocate of the role of the teacher in the teaching-learning process. He states,

> We teach who we are. . . . Teaching, like any truly human activity, emerges from one's inwardness, for better or worse. As I teach, I project the condition of my soul onto my students, my subject, and our way of being together. . . . In fact, knowing my students and my subject depends heavily on self-knowledge. When I do not know myself, I cannot know who my students are. . . .
>
> We need to open a new frontier in our exploration of good teaching: the inner landscape of a teacher's life. To chart that landscape fully, three paths must be taken—intellectual, emotional, and spiritual—and none can be ignored. Reduce teaching to intellect and it becomes a cold abstraction: reduce it to emotions and it becomes narcissistic; reduce it to the spiritual and it loses its anchor to the world. Intellect, emotion, and spirit depend on each other for wholeness. They are interwoven in the human self and in education at its best, and we need to interweave them in our pedagogical discourse as well. . . . Here is a secret hidden in plain sight: good teaching cannot be reduced to technique; good teaching comes from the identity and integrity of the teacher [1997, pp. 15–16].

What are the presumptions and implications of this image? First, this view of teaching stresses the necessity of every teacher to develop as a unique person. The sum of the specific human encounters between students and the teacher within a special community is the essence of education. Teachers are not to be equated with teaching technique.

Second, the academy—the collective faculty—is critical to judging the quality of teaching or, more accurately, the teacher. An appeal to a higher and powerful social and normative order that has its own intrinsic authority is implicit and should even be explicit according to Bellah (1998, 1999). Faculty are not just to serve student clients per se, but to pursue truth, to help fellow faculty develop within the community of scholars, to judge others for their contributions to the academy and to society, and to educate students about the value of life, the common good, and for a career if appropriate. Bellah (1999) argues that faculty are to "contribute to the self-understanding of society, so both individually and collectively we can make sense of our world" (p. 20). Higher education faculty are much more than employees of just another segment of our economy, responding only to external demands and succumbing to the tyranny of the free market.

Third, this image reflects an expanded definition of scholarship. Ernest Boyer, author of the influential book *Scholarship Defined* (1990), argues that faculty can be expected to be scholars and pursue scholarship in all they do. Only the specific outcomes of the work—teaching, research, or service— and the context and setting of the work differ. This perspective fosters the importance of colleges and universities in protecting and advancing the intellectual capital of the faculty. In *Scholarship Assessed* (Glassick, Huber, and Maeroff, 1997), the sequel to *Scholarship Defined* (Boyer, 1990), the authors propose that the evaluation of scholars include an assessment of their virtue and character. Their three elements of character—integrity, perseverance, and courage—overlap to a considerable degree with Parker Palmer's selection of identity and integrity as the critical moral criteria.

Learning communities are central to both perspectives. The student-centered image is based on a utilitarian argument of efficiency and effectiveness linked to the demands for external accountability. But learning communities are to foster learning in social skills, leadership, civic responsibility, teamwork, and problem solving as well. The teacher-centered image stresses the unique role of the academy in society, that is, the community of scholars. Both are concerned about student development, although the learning advocates may be likely to endorse the merits of service-learning and the symbiotic relationship between action and reflection. Those faculty with a traditional perspective consider contemplative thought as essential and sufficient to becoming an educated person (see Harkevy and Benson, 1998), but others, like Parker Palmer (1990), stress the importance of both action and reflection in learning and growing.

Both images rely on a purposeful union, a connectedness, a special relationship or community. I have used the term *purposeful union* to indicate that education is more than people just getting together. Community exists for a purpose—to develop people, to produce learning, to advance intellectual capital, and so forth. The nature of this union varies depending on the relative saliency of each element and the centrality of the content to be learned.

In his latest book, *The Courage to Teach* (1997), Palmer uses the concept of the community of truth as the integrative element to describe the teaching-learning process. The student and the teacher must be in a relationship with each other, but they must be connected in a special type of community—a community in which they are also relating to the subject. "The community of truth, far from being linear and static and hierarchical, is circular, interactive, and dynamic" (Palmer, 1997, p. 103). Only when both teacher and student are searching for truth together can they avoid the problems of absolutism or relativism and each partner's becoming too narcissistic or self-absorbed. The faculty member is not the only person who has access to truth, nor are the students as customers always correct. "In the community of truth, as in real life, there are no pristine objects of knowledge and ultimate authorities. . . . Education is more than delivering propositions about objects to passive audiences" (Palmer, 1997, p. 101).

By linking the teacher and the learner in a collaborative learning community, as both Barr and Tagg as well as Palmer do, the image of the teacher as the sage—the authority transmitting knowledge to passive students in a large lecture hall—almost entirely disappears. Palmer again provides insight into how we should look at teachers: "Community, or connectedness, is the principle behind good teaching, but different teachers with different gifts create community in surprisingly diverse ways, using widely divergent methods" (1997, p. 115). In sum, teaching is more than transmitting knowledge; good teaching touches and transforms people through relationships and community.

Implications for Assessment. What are the implications for assessing the work of professors, given the centrality of community linking the four elements—the teacher and teaching, and the learner and learning—in the teaching-learning process? I answer this general question by posing four related questions:

- Why do we assess?
- What are the standards and criteria of quality and effectiveness?
- What do we assess?
- How do we assess?

Why Do We Assess? In assessing the work of faculty, two goals usually are cited: to foster the development of faculty and to demonstrate accountability. Both images incorporate both goals, but the foci differ. Advocates of student learning emphasize accountability and improvement in learning more than the development of teachers as scholars. The stress is on improving teaching techniques to produce more learning, often within the context of simultaneously considering cost, access, and quality. Menges and Reyes use the words "learning productivity" to describe this image: "When learning productivity improves, student learning will increase in relation to its costs" (1997, p. 476). In short, assessment is based on instrumental and economic factors.

Advocates of the teacher's perspective have included accountability and faculty development as the reasons for evaluating teaching, but most often their focus is on improving one's teaching strategies and techniques—also largely instrumental issues. But higher education faculty need to get to know themselves better as individuals and as scholars. Parker Palmer observes, "I have worked with countless teachers, and many of them have confirmed my own experience: as important as methods may be, the most practical thing we can achieve in any kind of work is insight into what is happening inside us as we do it. The more familiar we are with our inner terrain, the more sure-footed our teaching—and living—becomes" (1997, pp. 20–21). Assessment from this viewpoint needs to take this aspect of teaching into account.

The focus of the evaluation of teaching has not been on the development of the soul of the teacher, that is, the identity and integrity of the professor as a person. Nor has the issue of intellectual capital been foremost in our dialogue and research. Assessment as a means to protect, promote, and foster intellectual capital—of both the individual and collective faculty—has not seemed of primary importance for us. Instead, we have been helping faculty become more efficient and effective in employing a spectrum of teaching techniques and skills, such as lecturing, testing, providing feedback, and questioning. Personal characteristics of faculty as correlates of student ratings and achievement have been well documented, but they more often are enthusiasm, knowledge of the subject matter, and gender rather than character, integrity, and identity. Both perspectives value evaluation, but the core of teaching—the teacher in a community of learning—has not been the primary rationale for the investment in assessment.

As the public becomes more and more educated (in a formal sense), the faculty collectively will need to communicate more effectively about their accountability to society. It may require greater attention to our implicit codes of ethics of professional standards and greater communication with our external audiences about the standards of learning and teaching. Because the call for accountability will not and should not disappear, we should work at integrating both purposes. Being accountable to society includes improving the quality of the work of the faculty.

What Are the Standards and Criteria of Quality and Effectiveness? This question asks us how we think about quality. The student-focused perspective defines the value of a faculty member's work in terms of influence and impact on the student. Years ago the phrase to describe this influence was "the whole student"; today the common phrase is "student outcomes," two words that reveal much about our views of the desired contribution of higher education to society (Braskamp and Braskamp, 1997). We have shifted to a utilitarian notion of excellence and value, a view that certainly has its merits. Including cost, equity, access, and quality all in the same equation forces us to compare the costs of different instructional delivery systems on the basis of the return of the investment. By doing so, we in higher education are responsible in being responsive to our larger community needs.

As technology becomes more prevalent in student learning, the evaluation of teaching also will need to expand its domain. This is appropriate and necessary. But as higher education becomes more and more an industry in which economic principles are the yardstick of value and worth, how will the scholarship and the personhood of a teacher be included in our equation of quality? If the evaluation of teaching includes an assessment of the person—the teacher—as one important element, we are entering controversial territory to be sure. Although we have not explicitly recognized such terms as *perseverance, integrity,* and *identity* in our evaluations to date, the academy has recognized them at least implicitly. For example, tenured faculty do not look kindly on an assistant professor who publishes little until the fifth year. With concern, they wonder if this professor will continue to publish once tenured; it is an issue of perseverance. Glassick, Huber, and Maeroff (1997) offer us this perspective:

> We would like to see these standards [of the work of the faculty] embedded in qualities of character that ensure that evaluation and all activities connected to scholarship, including faculty development and self-enrichment, have a moral dimension. . . . If higher education is to continue to help lead the nation, then surely its scholarly accomplishments, as laudable as they are, must be grounded in principles that speak to humankind's noblest aspects [1997, p. 67].

If we focus on the teacher, then faculty self-understanding and faculty contributions to the community of scholars and their fellow colleagues in their department or campus are important. We then must include these characteristics in assessment. If community is critical to learning and teaching, then we must base our judgments of quality of teaching on faculty contributions to build and support community and the work of their colleagues (Stake and Cisneros-Cohernour, 1998). We also must include in our evaluation the effectiveness of individual faculty collaborations with fellow faculty in such matters as developing discipline-related objectives of learning, support of interdisciplinary initiatives in curriculum, and contributions of one's teaching and instruction to the department's overall objectives and goals (Joe Cory, personal communication, 1998).

In sum, we need to solve better how to integrate the traditional values of the academy with the new challenges brought about by technology, collaboration and teamwork, and calls for greater accountability. If we wish faculty also to be scholars in their work in multiple communities (such as public intellectuals), we need to be more inclusive in our criteria and standards of quality. Neither a focus on only student learning nor only faculty development is sufficient.

What Do We Assess? What we assess emanates in large measure from our definition of quality. If learning is the most important element, measures of student performance are the cornerstone of the assessment. The consequential validity of student assessment then becomes important. However, the pendulum swing of student assessment to student learning outcomes may lead to a standardization of education without necessarily achieving high standards (Braskamp and Braskamp, 1997). As the need for accountability in a consumer-oriented education increases, the public (rightly or wrongly) is asking for a limited set of public indicators of student performance as the means of demonstrating the accountability of teachers. In this search, a paradox must be addressed: the more we concentrate on a single assessment strategy (test or measure of quality or effectiveness) to improve the quality of what is being assessed, the more likely the quality will decrease rather than increase. For example, if we focus too much on using student ratings of teaching to measure the quality of teaching, the quality of teaching in the aggregate on a campus will arguably be less effective. Faculty will likely become less diverse in their teaching styles, less sensitive to individual students needs, and less likely to try innovative teaching strategies. (Students often give instructors who try unique pedagogical strategies less favorable ratings.)

As teachers become partners in a team-based delivery system (as a presenter or a web designer, for example) that incorporates instructional technology, teacher-student and teacher-teacher relationships change. If the production of the content, the pedagogical strategies, and the delivery of the learning environment are done by different professionals, the individual faculty member no longer has total responsibility for educating the students. A faculty member, viewed as the one who engages in multiple tasking in his or her unique way, becomes an obsolete model. The challenges for assessment of team instruction and collaboration among faculty in the learning community are obvious. How do students assess the contributions of each teacher if many teachers are involved? What if the teacher has no personal contact with the students and does the teaching through chat space? How can one try to develop causal linkages among the various components of the learning environment and the unique contributions of each faculty member? Here community is especially significant, since collaboration among colleagues is the context in which colleagues influence and are influenced by each other.

How Do We Assess? The methods for collecting evidence from the available sources (among them, students, faculty themselves and their peers, and records) are related intrinsically to our views of the teaching-learning process. If we stress student learning, the focus is on student achievement measured reliably and even completed external to the teaching-learning process. Barr and Tagg argue, "The effectiveness of the assessment system for developing alternative learning environments depends in part upon its being external to learning programs and structures. . . . Ideally, an institution's assessment program would measure the 'value-added' over the course of students' experience at the college" (1995, p. 20). Monitoring student progress from entry until graduation demonstrates accountability to the relevant constituencies, and separating assessment of student learning from the teaching-learning process usually provides external credibility. However, this separation does not directly assist the teacher and student in the learning process on a continual basis.

If higher education continues to be increasingly consumer driven, with students assuming a larger role in determining the quality and effectiveness of their education, what are the major implications? Will the evaluation of teaching become too responsive to the needs of the consumer? Do the consumers know what is best to be taught and the kinds of experiences they need? Will higher education fall into a productivity trap, whereby the products (such as student credit hours or units of learning) become the criteria of quality and success? Will this lead to performance-based funding of individual faculty and institutions?

If we focus only on the teacher or teaching, we will not move beyond our current practices. Many of our student-based evaluation procedures aimed at evaluating the teacher and teaching methods seem out of date and out of touch. Student ratings, in particular, presume a pedagogical strategy of the master teacher's personally presenting knowledge to students—students who often are in a passive mode. Student ratings of teacher behavior rather than student learning have served as the primary criterion of the quality of the teaching-learning process. We need research to help us better understand the important features of the context of teaching—the community of truth, to use Palmer's phrase. Peer evaluation as currently designed comes closest because it involves peers, but to date the peers have focused almost exclusively on how their colleague as an individual is teaching. Such judgments still are personalized rather than dealing with the dynamics of the teaching-learning process within the community, the department, or the campus.

In our attempts to promote faculty development through assessment, we also have not given sufficient attention to the principle that faculty development occurs within a community, not in isolation. Although faculty are by and large internally motivated and become more self-referenced in their careers (Maehr and Braskamp, 1994), they still need the support and feedback of their peers to develop as scholars. Thus, peer evaluation needs to be an essential element in any evaluation of faculty. Parker Palmer argues, "The growth of any craft depends on shared practice and honest dialogue among the people who do it. . . . Good talk about good teaching is what we need—to enhance both our professional practice and the selfhood from which it comes" (1997, p. 144) Only faculty collectively have the experience and standards of scholarship that are both credible and useful to individual faculty. Peer evaluation does not violate academic freedom, but instead provides one of its best defenses. Judgment by peers is essential if faculty desire to enjoy their relative autonomy and self-governance.

Future Challenges

The overriding challenges for advocates of faculty assessment are quite evident. If we accept the premise that evaluation strategies reflect our views of the faculty member in the teaching-learning process, we can shape a dialogue related to the future of faculty assessment by addressing these issues.

Expand the Criteria of Excellence. As we begin to understand fully the changing role of the faculty member in American higher education, we need to take into account the issue of the changing interdependence among faculty. On the one hand, we need to preserve the tenets of the traditional academy, whereby a community of scholars works to build intellectual capital. Faculty individually and collectively must be scholars. They need to be judged by their scholarship and the extent to which they enhance the teaching effectiveness and scholarship of their colleagues. Stake and Cisneros-Cohernour (1998) point out the need to base the judgment of quality of teaching on faculty contributions to build and support community and advance the work of their colleagues.

On the other hand, we need to respond to the new market-driven forces in an increasingly competitive environment. In meeting these needs, faculty increasingly will become part of a team of experts. With technology playing an ever more important role in the delivery of instruction, teamwork among professionals will only increase. The single instructor performing multiple tasks gives way to a team approach. Collaboration and membership in a community increase in either case. Character here represents being a useful colleague who is dependable and shows respect for others.

Faculty in their conversations pointed to a complex portrayal of their work as professors. Once the person as teacher and scholar is included as part of the equation of quality, the relationship of the person to the community must be considered.

Use Merit and Worth to Denote Quality. We need to include both merit (the standards of the discipline) and worth (the contributions of a faculty member to the local campus and department) (Scriven, 1978) in our discussions and plans. In the past, faculty and administrators have not adequately examined the institutional context of teaching—the values of the local academy and the institutional mission. Too often we have assumed that a teacher is good—or not so good—in all places with all students. We cannot proceed much further in defining the quality of a professor's contributions through her or his teaching without addressing the larger issue of purpose of the institution. Mission is especially salient in colleges and universities that are centered on a religious or faith tradition.

Worth forces the members of any community to address the issue of institutional mission publicly. We thus need to emphasize the role of the faculty member as being place bound as well as discipline bound (John D. Edwards, personal communication, 1999). Being a member of a community is important, because part of the evaluation must include how each individual contributes to advancing the well-being of the institution. If we link quality only to the standards and values of the disciplines at the expense of the academy, we are dangerously undermining the authority of the academy in our society. A community of scholars at each institution must exercise its influence and morality beyond the disciplines represented if the collective faculty are to remain more than a segment of our economy.

Further Connect Faculty Assessment and Development. We can best increase the usefulness and utility of faculty assessment by building bridges between career development and evaluation. Assessment must include the life and career of a teacher in the academy. We need to establish measures of teacher behavior and values that reinforce the image that professors are persons called to some higher purpose—members of a local educational community with a specific mission. In my conversations with faculty, they often refer to their profession in terms beyond a career; it is a part of their life choices. Faculty with considerable experience often reflect on their past in their conversation, whereas faculty just beginning their work as faculty like to think in terms of a successful journey and one that will be of value to the larger community.

I think the metaphor "sitting beside" portrays this approach to evaluation. I have always believed that good assessment can build community—that is, "sitting beside" makes for good assessment. When faculty are working together, one first trying to understand the goals and desires of another as well as observing and evaluating the demonstration of teaching, the faculty colleague has a better perspective from which to provide feedback, evaluative as it is and must be. "Sitting beside" is different from "standing over," the more frequent posture in faculty evaluation.

An expansion of the current thinking about assessment, which focuses too much on the methods of collecting evidence, is needed. Good assessment begins with setting and negotiating two sets of expectations: the expectations a faculty member has of the institution to advance his or her career and the institution's expectations such as the requirements and standards of performance for the faculty. The faculty and administrators responsible for communicating the institution's expectations need to communicate the values and standards—what is considered acceptable work—and how that work is to be evaluated—what evidence is considered credible and reliable to be used in judging the contributions of a faculty member. At a practical level, it will require a more significant role of colleagues, particularly the departmental chair or college dean. The chair and the faculty member jointly need to agree on what is expected and what evidence is needed to demonstrate one's contribution. This is critical if identity, character, and the "teacher" are to be considered important elements in the assessment process. The chair or dean plays a critical role in communicating the results of the assessment; the assessment needs to have consequences if it is to be useful. Faculty need to gain an understanding of their "worth" and "merit" through evaluation, and learn of their status within their institution. Tierney (1999) recommends a performance contract—a formal negotiated arrangement with consequences to highlight the seriousness of the assessment to both the institution and the individual.

Refocus How We Assess Excellence in Teaching. This is the area of best practices, which is based on experiences and practical wisdom aided by research. The focus should be on the how to implement peer evaluations. This strategy of faculty's judging others is growing in popularity. However, no single or easy procedure or set of guidelines, such as those we have developed for administrating student surveys, now exists, and we should not expect or aim for any singular method or strategy. The more we incorporate the teacher as an important element in the assessment process, the more we will need to rely on informed and thoughtful judgements of peers. This is a difficult challenge. From my experience, faculty, especially at smaller institutions, are reluctant to judge others. Ironically, the strong relationships and a strong sense of community prevent them from being objective and honest. Thus, measures to ensure fairness and neutrality for the common and larger good need to be part of the assessment process.

Accept the Tension of Faculty's Being Both Responsive and Responsible. As the marketplace and technology play a more central role in instruction and learning, the role of the faculty member as an individual member of the academy takes on a new meaning. The challenge is to figure out how to evaluate faculty within this new context, a context filled with external accountability demands, technological advances, student needs often at variance with the lifestyle and values of the faculty, and diversity of institutional missions. In short, the future of students must be taken into account, and faculty cannot assume any longer that only they know what is best for the student. The agenda of higher education must be the result of negotiation and collaboration among the various and diverse communities of interest (Braskamp and Wergin, 1998).

If the academy becomes too responsive to market forces and the bottom line, however, the result will be a lack of responsibility. That is, the academy may not have sufficient autonomy or the authority to build its intellectual capital to serve society (Braskamp, 1997). Bellah (1999) puts it this way: "What is freedom in the market is tyranny in other spheres, such as the professions and politics. A decent society depends on the autonomy of the spheres" (p. 19). How can the evaluation of teaching advance the values of the academy, such as the pursuit of truth and the faculty member as a scholar? The newly formed Carnegie Teaching Academy, jointly sponsored by the American Association for Higher Education and the Carnegie Foundation for the Advancement of Teaching, reinforces the desire to honor teaching as a scholarly activity. Through this support, communities of teachers as scholars will be able to share and learn from their colleagues both within and outside their discipline. The importance of "being there" is emphasized over "having been there." This strategy recognizes that one cannot learn or evaluate fully from a distance but must witness, experience, and be a part of the community. Since teaching has been viewed, practiced, and evaluated in large part as a private matter, we need to continue to advance recent attempts to help faculty better understand how to assess the teaching of others, including team and collaborative teaching, service-learning, and team and collaborative learning.

Improve Communication Among the Stakeholders. Finally, we need to understand better the notion of talking power to truth (Robinson, 1998). Professors and administrators have ignored the research findings on faculty assessment. They have questioned the "truth" of the researchers and experts as they have defined the assessment process, and perhaps for good reason at times. As Robinson argues, "Local problems can not be subsumed under the theoretical problems of the researcher" (1998, p. 4). Researchers and faculty active in assessment will benefit greatly by becoming a member of the "community of truth," to use Palmer's phrase, even though they may be quite uncomfortable in taking on this responsibility. In my conversations with faculty, I find that they are pleasantly surprised about their engagement in the topic of assessment and their ability to discuss easily with other faculty they do not know well or have not met before. It reflects the highly personal nature of the topic, because assessment of work is often meant to be assessment of the person as well. For this reason, we need to develop communication modes, such as small groups, to discuss this issue. It also means redefining the practice of assessment as being less of a scientific exercise and viewing it as an argument supported with credible evidence. It is process that stresses clarification, truth seeking, and understanding rather than a delivery of objectivity and truth. Good assessment focuses discussion.

Conclusion

Our primary goal in faculty assessment remains to improve the scholarship of the faculty. To do so, we must keep these points in mind. First, the context of the work of the faculty must be given greater import. We have the obligation to meet societal expectations, that is, being responsive to our external communities as we at the academy—itself a unique community—foster and develop faculty as responsible scholars. The work of a faculty member is now more complex, more collaborative, and more responsive to societal needs. The communities within and without the academy must intersect. Second, just as our responsiveness should increase, so must our responsibility as scholars. Glassick, Huber, and Maeroff (1997) believe that "the assessment of scholarship begins not with procedures but with ideals" (p. 66). Being both responsive and responsible does not mean returning to the traditional academy. To change is not merely to accede to the critics who are intent in their questioning of the academy's relevance, efficiency, effectiveness, and contributions to society. Instead, we must change in a way that best meets the changing needs of our world and the changing social interactions and structure of doing the work of the academy.

Third, when we assess our work, we must rethink and rearrange the way we combine the elements of teacher and teaching, learner and learning into the assessment process. Just as we cannot return as a collective faculty to the academy of the past, we cannot assess the work of the individual faculty member as we have in the past. Instead we must begin with community to reinforce the context of the purposeful union of students and faculty in the learning process. Moreover, we must use community in assessment, since it is the primary means to assess the work of the faculty. Assessment must focus on student learning, but good assessment of the work of the faculty is more than that. At its core is the worth and integrity of the individual faculty as a member of a community that still enjoys a unique status in a free and democratic society. Our goal is to maintain this status.

Notes

1. *Evaluation* and *assessment* both refer to a process of judging quality, effectiveness, value, worth, and merit for the purposes of improvement and accountability. When I refer to faculty evaluation and assessment, I include the entire process of three inter-related activities: determining faculty expectations; collecting evidence from a variety of sources, such as self, faculty colleagues, students, and records, and using a variety of methods and strategies; and both assisting the faculty member to grow personally and professionally and assisting the institution in making decisions about the faculty member's salary and promotion and tenure status (Braskamp and Ory, 1994).

2. This chapter is a somewhat personal perspective of the art and assessment of teaching. I developed the first section on "Elements of Assessment" during the 1997–98 academic school year when I was a faculty member at the University of Illinois at Chicago, after a departure from the faculty ranks for twenty-four years as an administrator at four different institutions. I identified what I consider to be the major of elements of assessing teaching.

I primarily relied on two personal experiences as I wrote this section. I reflected on *Assessing Faculty Work,* which I coauthored with John Ory, in which we defined assessment as "sitting beside," with an emphasis on faculty development. Before someone can judge someone else, she must first understand the other person. Although we did not use the language of Parker Palmer (1997) of "listening to the teacher within," I think that idea was implicit, although certainly not well thought out. But the bias or tendency to treat each professor as a unique individual before judging her or her work was at least latent in our thinking.

The second is the fact that I was a professor the year (1997–98) I wrote the first part of this chapter. I spent considerable time thinking about how to influence student learning; I seemed often obsessed by it that year. When I taught a course titled "Assessment and Accountability" in the fall semester, I worked very hard at focusing on the students and not on my teaching techniques or myself as a person. In the course evaluations, a comment from one student was significant: "I wish he would have expressed more of his opinions." This reinforced my own self-assessment that I perhaps was too bland, too mechanical, and too hesitant to reveal myself in class.

During second semester, I taught a course titled "The Academic Profession," and I was much more willing to be myself. I enjoyed teaching more, and I was willing to rely on and defend my own perspective of my inner sense of self-worth. I did not rely solely on student learning or opinion to judge my work as a teacher. In both classes that year, I kept coming back to this question: "Are the students learning anything and developing as persons?" As a professor, I was reminded that I enjoyed teaching more when I viewed myself as a unique person with something to contribute, while remaining firmly committed to focusing on what the students are learning—attitudes not always easily reconciled. It is this paradox that I think lies at the heart of teaching. Can what seems to be a contradiction for many be evaluated? The first part of this chapter is devoted to answering this rhetorical question.

In July 1998, I became the chief academic officer at Loyola University Chicago. As a Jesuit university, Loyola has a long tradition of stressing intellectual rigor, serving others, and caring for others—*cura personalis*—and advocacy of social justice shapes the culture of the campus. The mission statement of Loyola Chicago opens with this statement: "Knowledge in the service of others." As a Catholic university, the faculty are concerned about the issue of character because of *Ex Corde Ecclesiae,* the 1990 document from Pope John Paul II, who desires Catholic universities to renew their allegiance to the Catholic tradition (Zech, 1999). For example, it specifies that faculty exhibit "integrity of doctrine and good character."

References

Barr, R. B., and Tagg, J. "From Teaching to Learning—A New Paradigm for Undergraduate Education." *Change,* Nov.–Dec. 1995, pp. 13–25.

Bellah, R. N. "Freedom and Responsibility." Invited address presented at the annual meeting of the American Council on Education, San Francisco, 1998.

Bellah, R. N. "Freedom, Coercion, and Authority." *Academe,* 1999, 85, 17–21.

Boyer, E. L. (1990). *Scholarship Reconsidered: Priorities of the Professoriate.* San Francisco: Jossey-Bass.

Braskamp, L. A. *On Being Responsive and Responsible.* Washington, D.C.: Council for Higher Education Accreditation, 1997.

Braskamp, L. A., and C. Braskamp, D. C. *The Changing Pendulum of Standards and Evidence.* Washington, D.C.: Council for Higher Education Accreditation, 1997.

Braskamp, L. A., and Ory, J. C. *Assessing Faculty Work.* San Francisco: Jossey-Bass, 1994.

Braskamp, L. A., and Wergin, J. F. "Forming New Social Partnerships." In William G. Tierney (ed.), *The Responsive University: Restructuring for High Performance.* Baltimore: Johns Hopkins University Press, 1998.

Ewell, P. T. "Organizing for Learning." *AAHE Bulletin,* 1997, 50(4), 3–6.

Glassick, C. E., Huber, M. T., and Maeroff, G. I. *Scholarship Assessed: Evaluation of the Professoriate.* San Francisco: Jossey-Bass, 1997.

Harkevy, I., and Benson, L. "Ed-Platonizing and Democratizing Education as the Bases of Service Learning." In R. A. Rhoads and J.P.F. Howard (eds.), *Academic Service Learning: A Pedagogy of Action and Reflection.* New Directions for Teaching and Learning, no. 73. San Francisco: Jossey-Bass, 1998.

Maehr, M. L., and Braskamp, L. A. *The Motivation Factor: A Theory of Personal Investment.* San Francisco: New Lexington Press, 1994.

McKeachie, W. J. "Good Teaching Makes a Difference—and We Know What It Is." In R. P. Perry and J. C. Smart (eds.), *Effective Teaching in Higher Education: Research and Practice.* New York: Agathon Press, 1997.

Menges, R. J., and Reyes. E. A. "Quality Indicators for Teaching and Learning." In K. Strydom, L.O.K. Lategan, and A. Muller (eds.), *Enhancing Institutional Self-Evaluation and Quality in the South African University System.* Bloemfontein, Republic of South Africa: Unit for Research into Higher Education, University of the Orange Free State, 1997.

Palmer, P. J. *The Active Life: A Spirituality of Work, Creativity, and Caring.* New York: HarperCollins, 1990.

Palmer, P. J. *The Courage to Teach.* San Francisco: Jossey-Bass, 1997.

Robinson, V.M.J. "Methodology and the Research-Practice Gap." *Educational Researcher,* 1998, 27, 17–26.

Scriven, M. "Value Versus Merit." *Evaluation News,* 1978, 8, 1–3.

Shulman, L. S. "Taking Learning Seriously." *Change,* 1999, 31, 11–17.

Stake, R. E., and Cisneros-Cohernour, E. J. "Evaluation of College Teaching in a Community of Practice." Paper presented at the annual meeting of the American Educational Research Association, San Diego, 1998.

Tierney, W. G. *The Responsive University.* San Francisco: Jossey-Bass, 1999.

Zech, C. "The Faculty and Catholic Institutional Identity." *America,* May 22, 1999, pp. 11–15.

LAWRENCE A. BRASKAMP *is chief academic officer of Loyola University Chicago.*

4

The advent of technology-assisted teaching calls for a new way of thinking about teaching and its evaluation.

Technology, Evaluation, and the Visibility of Teaching and Learning

Randall J. Bass

In this chapter, I address three questions: How do new technology environments affect teaching and learning in ways that have implications for evaluation? How might technology tools be used to help facilitate the representation and evaluation of teaching? What are some of the issues that institutions should consider in evaluating faculty work with teaching and technology?

My interest in these questions began very personally. In 1998, without a traditional record of scholarship—in fact without a single traditional refereed article—I received tenure at a university that requires such things, on a case built almost entirely on work with new media technologies and the scholarship of teaching and learning. Along the way, I experienced many of the vicissitudes that characterize faculty work in new environments and doing nontraditional work. Many of my endeavors with technology went awry, sometimes as a result of things out of my control. I experienced a precipitous drop in teaching evaluations in my first immersive semester of teaching with technology, I felt a sense of isolation of having no colleagues or mentors doing similar work, and I know the difficulty and stress of translating seemingly unfamiliar work for an audience of colleagues as part of the tenure process. All in all, choosing a nontraditional path meant that my journey to tenure was a pretty uncomfortable one. I am recalling it here not

---

Note: Portions of this chapter were adapted from "Discipline and Publish: Technology, Faculty Work, and Accountability," presented at the 1999 Forum on Faculty Roles and Rewards, of the American Association for Higher Education, San Diego, California (http://www.georgetown.edu/bassr/disc&pub.html).

so that I can vent about it, but because the ways in which it was uncomfortable are emblematic for the future of higher education. They bear on both the integration of new technologies and the evaluation of teaching as intellectual work in the academy.

Over the same years that my journey to tenure was taking place, I was spending a lot of time working with faculty across the country on ways to use and think about the integration of technology into teaching. Over the past seven years, both on my own and in collaboration with other projects, I have worked with perhaps as many as a thousand faculty from a few hundred colleges and universities. In this work I have developed some sense of the impact of technology on faculty work and the willingness and unwillingness of faculty to bring new technologies into their professional lives. Over this time, I have been moved by the willingness of some faculty to do new things, engage in new kinds of work, and test pedagogical innovations, and at the same time the constraints on those desires—by both the institutional environment and teachers' own self-policing.

Faculty are unable or reluctant to revise, restructure, and reinvent in the light of new technologies for several reasons, two of which bear directly on the issue of teaching evaluation. First, they recognize the time and energy involved and are skeptical that the significant effort required to undertake innovation with technology will be rewarded in ways comparable to other kinds of work (let alone that they might be penalized if their student evaluations go down). And second, and more subtle, faculty are at a loss to know how to press ahead with technology-enhanced pedagogies because we know so little about the underlying processes of teaching and learning and because the environments in which we are trained, and for the most part in which we do our work, condescend to the idea of paying attention to these processes as legitimate objects of investigation. This is an intrinsic quality of the academy, and it becomes internalized by us, its practitioners, despite our best intentions otherwise.

I begin with the connection between innovation and evaluation in order to highlight the two versions of the question, How do we evaluate and reward faculty for their work with new technologies? On the one hand, this question arises in the context of the pioneer and early adopter faculty who are doing innovative work—with pedagogy or scholarly publication—in electronic environments and the need to recognize that work in the evaluation and reward process. This is the first version of the question: How do we support those who have chosen to work with new tools in new environments? On the other hand, the question is becoming almost ubiquitous among institutions that are trying to encourage their faculty to experiment with and adopt new technologies, either as part of place-based classroom instruction or distance- and distributed-learning initiatives. This is the other version of the question: How do we get more faculty interested in changing their practice? In this, the evaluation and reward process is one key obstacle for faculty interest, as institutions discover that they have the very faculty whom the system created: faculty with neither time, training, nor institutional incentives to examine their teaching systematically and to adopt technology-enhanced innovations in practice thoughtfully.

Although interrelated, there is a difference between the problem of recognizing and evaluating innovation, and institutionalizing innovation through evaluation and reward procedures in ways that accommodate transformations in the learning environment. I address both of these needs by looking at the relationship of technology, teaching, and evaluation in three ways.

First, I look at three areas of impact that interactive technologies have on teaching and learning with a bearing on the evaluation of teaching:

- The public nature of teaching and learning in new environments and the implications of that visibility on evaluation
- The heightened emphasis on process and interactivity created by new learning environments
- The consequent shift in faculty roles as they take on new tasks of designing and managing whole learning environments

Second, I briefly look at three different ways that technologies might be of use in the evaluation of teaching:

- The capacities of new media tools to provide information about student learning behaviors, or what we might call "computer use metadata"
- The use of electronic tools to facilitate assessment and feedback, and to engage students more fully in the evaluation process, perhaps even as an integral part of their own learning
- The use of electronic environments to enable the reflective representation of the complexities of the teaching and learning process better, including such methods as the hypertext course portfolio and multimedia case studies

And finally, I conclude with a short list of broad issues that I believe institutions should consider when trying to revise teaching evaluation procedures in the light of new learning environments:

- Embedding teaching evaluation in a context of inquiry and intellectual work
- Revising evaluation instruments and procedures to focus more flexibly on interactivity and changing faculty roles
- Seeing teaching (and teaching evaluation) not merely in individual contexts but communally and ecologically

I explore these areas of impact as answers to my three opening questions.

How Do New Technology Environments Affect Teaching and Learning in Ways That Have Implications for Evaluation?

In order to evaluate something, you have to be able to see it, and there is perhaps no greater impact of new technologies on the educational environment than their capacity to make both learning and reflective teaching visible. In myriad ways, interactive technologies create a more visible record of student learning, whether through the use of electronic discussion lists, bulletin boards, or Web-based communication environments; the use of electronic portfolios or publicly accessible student constructive projects; or the creation of collaborative, ongoing, digital projects stretching over multiple courses. If the evaluation of teaching ultimately rests on the evaluation of learning, then the heightened visibility of student learning has the potential to alter the forms and processes of teaching evaluation. As Joan DeGuire North asks,

> If one's expanded view of teaching includes evidence of influencing student learning, how does one document success at this new challenge? Learning over what period of time? What kind of learning: intellectual, social, attitudinal? Do all students have to learn the same content or can variations occur? Do we need to measure the strength of the faculty influence itself or just the outcome, however it was achieved (cause and effect)? Do we take into account that some learners are more ready than others, so that teaching is easier for some of us than others? Where would we look for evidence of effective learning? [North, 1999, pp. 186–187].

At the very least, new learning environments multiply the ways that evidence of student learning becomes accessible. In addition to traditional outcome measures and performances (such as quizzes, exams, and papers), new learning environments make it possible to examine the records of discussions, of students' "rehearsing" and developing complex ideas, and of students' collaborating and developing their knowledge in distributed ways. Much more is also possible to be learned regarding student usage of course materials, such as being able to track how often and in what ways students use on-line resources, take self-paced exams, or successfully solve practice problems.

Moreover, the creation of visible and accessible records of learning makes it possible as it has not been before to engage students in metacognitive activities in which developing critical perspectives on their own learning (or the learning of their peers) becomes an integral part of their subject-based learning. This new, heightened accessibility to the evidence of learning can have an impact as part of the fabric of any course. So too can it become the basis for wholly inventive approaches to student learning. For example, the University of Texas, Austin, project known as the On-line

Learning Record (OLR) makes student learning in a writing program accessible not only to teachers but to students themselves (Syverson, 1999). They learn to track their own progress, think about what it means to look at evidence of learning, and determine how to argue that evidence in the context of learning goals. The database of student learning and their analytic work with it become as important a text as any other in the multiple courses that use the OLR. The On-line Learning Record is one vivid example of the possibilities of making learning visible and how it substantively changes the terms of learning and blurs the boundary between teaching and learning.

How this bears on the evaluation of teaching depends a lot on what one means by teaching. Is teaching the content of the course, or the process and interaction of its unfolding? Is it the materials of instruction, or the aggregation of instructional moments? Is it a product or a process? In the words of Lee Shulman, "Too often teaching is identified only as the active interactions between teacher and students in a classroom setting (or even a tutorial session). I would argue that teaching, like other forms of scholarship, is an extended process that unfolds over time" (Shulman, 1998, p. 5). Whatever one's definition, teaching, and the faculty work associated with it in its extended processes, is much more visible when it makes extensive use of new technologies.

In thinking about this, I have found it useful to consider the distinction between two kinds of work in which faculty engage: the *local* and the *cosmopolitan*. Faculty spend most of their time engaged in local work— teaching, advising, committee service, and so forth. Yet in many institutions, a significant part of the reward process (and in some cases a disproportionate weight in the reward process) is based on cosmopolitan work: scholarship, research, publication, and other nationally visible work. Such work is cosmopolitan because it is visible, public, portable, and appropriable by other people in the field. When teaching goes on-line and is made publicly accessible through new media, the line between local and cosmopolitan work becomes blurred.

New media technologies make teaching public and cosmopolitan in a number of ways. Many courses that are taught on-line become "public" and in some respects "published." (This was almost invariably the case in the early and mid-1990s, when most on-line courses were published in open-platform Web environments; increasingly courses are conducted in partially closed password-protected course delivery environments, which has changed their status somewhat.) Nonetheless, most courses continue to be at least hybrid packages with some public, "world-readable" materials, often mixing curricular and scholarly material. The Web also offers a growing number of vehicles for instructors to make their public work with teaching widely accessible to others. One example is a resource like the World Lecture Hall, an extensive index to courses on the Web, where faculty can "self-publish" and disseminate their own on-line course materials. The courses pointed to on the Web through resources like the World Lecture Hall vary from simple collections of teaching materials, syllabi, quizzes, and so forth to more extensive "whole courses on-line." Such courses offer complete packages of content and course materials, including tutorials and study guides. And there are courses where not only the materials are available for public consumption but the actual unfolding process of the course, complete with views into the on-line interactive communication spaces or student constructive projects. In these cases, teaching, as both content and process, becomes publicly accessible.

Even in semipublic course delivery environments, on-line teaching unfolds in ways that make its peer review and evaluation very different from what was possible (or practical) in traditional environments, such as in the pilot peer review project of the Web Initiative for Teaching (WIT) in the University of Maryland system. In looking at a series of on-line, communication-intensive courses, the WIT Peer Review process attempts to keep process and interactivity at the center. Each instructor was asked to locate two peer reviewers for the project. In early instructions to peer reviewers they stated:

> Unlike a face-to-face classroom, the Web-enabled virtual classroom is open for your observations throughout the semester at your convenience. We are asking that you make an initial visit to the course website at the beginning of the semester, acquainting yourself with the syllabus and structure of the course, visiting the interactive conferencing, and testing the ease and logic of navigation around the Web course site. . . .
>
> Asynchronous discussions unfold over time. We would like to have you visit the course for an entire week at least twice in order to observe the pacing and style of learning interactions. An alternative might be to select and follow a module from the beginning to the end. Some of you may "shadow" the course on a weekly basis throughout the semester. The key is that you observe sufficiently to get an accurate reading of the quality of the interaction between the instructor and the students, and among the students [e-mail correspondence, Sept. 1999].

As part of the review process, the organizers ask the peer reviewers to follow a format outline for reports that analyzes three main areas: "quality of course content, the courseware environment and this particular learning experience." The format outline then goes on to detail these categories of address:

Part One: Review of the Course Itself
Course rationale
Goals and objectives
Instructional design
Learning and teaching theory
Responsiveness of learner needs
Learning and teaching strategies and activities
Content (discipline specific)
Interactivity

Use of mediate resources and the Web
Assessment, evaluation, and mastery
Accessibility, robustness, and technical support
Navigation
Internal organization and consistency

*Part Two: Review of Current Delivery of the Course
and Recommendations*
Instructor's role and teaching effectiveness
Recommendation for improvement

The WIT peer review has several interesting and noteworthy dimensions, including an emphasis on process and interactivity, attention to multiple levels of design (interface design, instructional design), attention to the learning and teaching theory behind the design and curriculum, attention to the ways the instructor meaningfully integrates digital tools and resources with the course content, and a general approach to course evaluation that takes the course in its overall environment.

As a peer reviewer in the program, I was mindful of several needs and gaps the process raised. First, I realized what a limited vocabulary we have for talking about the nuances of interactivity and knowledge-building processes (as opposed to the assessment of knowledge products), especially in the context of disciplinary thinking. Second, I was struck by how the instructor's pedagogy and design were circumscribed by the options made available in the course environment and that it was not always easy to tell where the teacher's intentional design stopped and the preestablished environment began. Finally, I realized how much there needed to be a reflective dimension built in to the digital environment, through which the instructor could communicate her rationale to me, the reviewer, about why certain choices had been made, or how the course's unfolding was and was not working within its design. There was, in the multilayered digital environment, no capacity for the faculty member to create a reflective commentary, rationale, or argument. In this respect, it is clear that one enormous need in higher education is the development of ancillary reflection and analysis tools to complement whole course environments. Such tools are necessary if we are to develop teacher evaluation processes that truly capture the complexity of learning in new environments.

How Might Technology Tools Be Used to Help Facilitate the Representation and Evaluation of Teaching?

There are at least three ways that technology tools can be used to facilitate the evaluation of teaching: through the electronically enhanced collection of data on student learning behavior in online environments, through online classroom assessment and feedback tools, and in representing the complexity of teaching as a process. How students use technology tools and resources largely determines the impact of technology on their learning. Therefore, a key component in assessing and representing student learning as evidence of effective teaching is the gathering of data on the ways that students make use of resources in new learning environments.

Electronic tools can be used for gathering quantitative data on student use. Many of these tools come built in to course management and delivery systems; still others require the help of campus technology support specialists to customize for local use. With these tools, instructors can learn how much use students are making of on-line resources, how many times particular documents or tutorials are accessed, how long students are using programs for particular sessions, and what patterns and frequency of use and participation are occurring in on-line spaces (for both individual students and whole classes). Such information is not evidence of learning per se, but metadata in that it complements the evidence of learning and student attitudes toward their learning environments.

Such metadata are deepened by electronic tools (and nonelectronic techniques) that engage students much more actively in classroom assessment and in the evaluation of their own learning and learning experience. In a recent essay, Devorah Lieberman (1999) surveys electronic tools for assessment and evaluation, listing such tools as electronic versions of TechnoCATs (technology-based Classroom Assessment Techniques), electronic versions of the Small Group Instructional Diagnosis, and the Flashlight Student Inventory. These types of tools are useful only in the broader context of faculty reflection on learning. And although tools like Flashlight are collective evaluation tools, tools for metadata and formative assessment generally must remain for the use of instructors as part of their own developmental processes. As Lieberman puts it, "Such tools, if used for evaluative purposes, might weaken an instructor's desire to ascertain student learning in relation to particular teaching strategies and might also discourage midcourse modification" (p. 145).

Electronic tools can also serve teaching evaluation by providing new, powerful tools for the representation of teaching as an argument about the relationship between student learning and pedagogy. I grappled with this issue in the preparation of my own tenure case as I searched for ways to present my technology-enhanced teaching. My solution was the creation of a hypertext course portfolio focusing on one specific, reconstructed course (Bass, 1998). Although the hypertext format was important to the representation of my teaching, the primary dimension of the reflection was choosing the form of a course portfolio in which I could present a single course (with its design and execution) as a kind of hypothesis testing that a certain kind of organization and collection of materials would produce a certain kind of learning. A course portfolio allowed me to investigate my own teaching not as a static collection of artifacts or as the production of traditional outcomes, but as an argument that unfolded in space and time.

There are many affinities between the idea of a course portfolio and a digital hypertext presentational environment. For example, the argument of a course (that is, a singular line of thought) counterbalances nicely with the many layers of material, context, and process that constitute any course. Representing a course that uses electronic environments in an electronic environment allows a kind of three-dimensional accounting that makes visible both the story of a course and its web of contexts. Creating a course portfolio in hypertext helped me address a number of issues endemic to the representation of teaching for evaluation:

Evidence. One of the salient problems of course portfolios and teaching portfolios is the problem of evidence. How much evidence do you include for your readers? If there is too much, the portfolio is overwhelming; too little runs the risk of leaving readers with questions or skepticism. A hypertext format allowed me to offer examples of evaluations and student learning in summary form and through representative samples and then present readers with direct electronic access links to the entire body of evidence.

Multiple modes of organization. The choice of a hypertext environment also gave me the luxury of multiple modes of organization and access. For example, the first section, entitled "Contexts," discusses the personal, institutional, and disciplinary contexts for the course. One can easily imagine constructing different paths through a course portfolio based on audience. An outside peer reviewer from the subject field might take a path oriented toward unique and innovative applications of disciplinary knowledge; an internal reviewer might follow a different hypertextual path oriented toward institutional mission or documentation of a new general education course in the context of its pilot implementation, or even the representation of an individual's progress in professional development. In other words, if *argument* implies *audience,* then a hypertext environment allows multiple approaches to both.

Courses in cohort contexts. A hypertext reflective environment also accentuates the capacity to point to other cohort courses on the Web with related interests or purposes. One can do that on paper, but it is much more vivid and immediate if there exist direct hypertext links from parts of the argument to similar courses on-line. As more and more curriculum goes on-line, this kind of hypertext "dialogue" among courses and electronic projects will help promote such work as community property.

Multiple layers of rationale. Finally, I used a tool I call an annotated syllabus (another uniquely electronic feature), in which the course syllabus was annotated with reflections about key moments of the course, accessible in pop-up windows where the syllabus and reflection are on the screen simultaneously. The annotated syllabus provides the main narrative of the portfolio that unfolds chronologically, tying each reflection electronically to a place in the syllabus.

One of the points to stress here is the real affinity between the public and hybrid nature of new media technologies and the principles of the scholarship of teaching and learning. The idea of a scholarship of teaching argues that there is not merely a scholarly component in teaching, but also a kind of scholarship in which teachers can engage with their own teaching. As Lee Shulman puts it, "For an activity to be designated as scholarship, it should manifest at least three key characteristics: it should be *public,* susceptible to *critical review and evaluation,* and accessible for *exchange and use* by other members of one's scholarly community" (1998, p. 5). As we have seen, new technologies can encourage and display faculty work in directions congruent with all three of these characteristics.

The force of a scholarship of teaching has impact on the nature of teaching both intrinsically—through the nature of the pedagogical argument—and extrinsically, in the capacity for "exchange and use." To quote Lee Shulman one more time:

> How many professional educators, when engaged in creating new course or a new curriculum, can turn to a published peer-reviewed scholarship of teaching in which colleagues at other colleges and universities present their experiments, their field trials, or their case studies of instruction and its consequences? Where is the scholarly literature through which higher educators study exemplars of teaching and can build upon that work? With precious few exceptions, we don't have such a literature [Shulman, 1999, p. 16].

While there must be institutional contexts that foster and value such a "literature" of teaching "exemplars," new technology environments are already proving themselves to be key agents in making reflective teaching public and accessible for exchange and use. This is happening in several ways through new technology environments, especially the Internet and World Wide Web, by providing a space for "publishing" teaching materials and making learning processes visible; enabling hybrid projects that breach traditional boundaries of teaching, scholarship, and service; and providing new means for peer reviewing and disseminating teaching materials as intellectual products: An example of the last point that expresses even further the cosmopolitan nature of curriculum published on the Internet is the Virtual Geography Department. A project funded by the National Science Foundation out of University of Texas, Austin, the Virtual Geography Department is not only a place where geography teachers and students can access resources related to the geography curriculum; it is also a place where geography faculty from any institution can contribute curriculum modules. When a teacher contributes a module, it is sent to an editorial group according to what kind of geography it is. That group vets it initially and, on approval, puts the module in a testing area, inviting geography teachers around the world to test and use it. When the module has received feedback and been revised, it is then put in the curriculum library and made a permanent part of the on-line materials.

We have just begun to see the possibilities not only of using public on-line spaces for exchanging, reviewing, and publishing teaching materials, but in the creation of new genres of teaching resources and processes and new forms of curriculum materials and knowledge environments that broaden what it means to evaluate teaching. Similarly, we are just beginning to see ways for using tools to allow teachers to represent the layers and processes of teaching for the evaluation process, through multimedia case study analyses, teacher-scholar webs that link faculty teaching work over time, collective digital archives of teaching materials, and reflections where faculty connect their work in courses to other cohort courses in local, disciplinary, and national contexts. These tools for representation are impossible to imagine apart from the evolution of a culture of inquiry and the elevation of teaching evaluation above accountability to a different level of respect for it as intellectual and integrative work. If the scholarship of teaching is intended to help treat matters of teaching and learning as subjects of intellectual inquiry—and thereby make the intellectual work of teaching and learning more visible—then new technology environments are a key tool of and agent for that visibility.

What Are Some of the Issues That Institutions Should Consider in Evaluating Faculty Work with Teaching and Technology?

The idea that new technologies help making teaching more visible highlights one of the trenchant differences between scholarship and teaching. Visibility in one's scholarship, one's professional repute, or the capacity of a faculty member to raise the visibility of his or her institution is something to be desired. In scholarship, the field of visibility is the engine behind faculty productivity in scholarship and research; that is, the idea of "being watched" motivates and structures faculty work, but it also limits and disciplines the kind of work they do. With teaching, visibility has generally been closely tied to accountability, and often in negative ways. Traditionally, one's teaching is institutionally visible under only one of two conditions: it is visible to students, and then public through their course evaluations and the scrutiny of those evaluations in the reward process; and it is visible when it is being watched and evaluated by colleagues for review, often in an invasive and uncomfortable process. In this sense, teaching gets doubly stigmatized. First, it holds a distant second place in graduate training to content and method; and then in employment, even in largely teaching institutions and where good teaching is highly valued, the close tie between visibility and accountability often narrows and inhibits faculty innovation and the way it is regarded as an intellectual enterprise.

In 1997 there was circulating on the Internet an essay by the historian David Noble called "Digital Diploma Mills," which was something of a jeremiad against the technologizing of the higher education curriculum, which he primarily understood as the process of "putting courses on-line." Ranging from healthy skepticism to paranoia, Noble's essay raises the specter of the Internet as an administrative instrument of surveillance:

> Once faculty and courses go on-line, administrators gain much greater direct control over faculty performance and course content than ever before and the potential for administrative scrutiny, supervision, regimentation, discipline and even censorship increase dramatically. . . . The technology also allows for much more careful administrative monitoring of faculty availability, activities, and responsiveness.

This is visibility as accountability with a vengeance. For Noble, making teaching visible through the Internet leads inevitably to commodification, surveillance, and control. When teaching and learning go public, there is the possibility for more administrative control and observation, and possibly a policing of content and process in ways that were difficult when left primarily to the private space of the classroom. But even if we grant some possibility to Noble's fears, I think we have seen that by making faculty work (and student learning) visible, new technologies can offer more than merely an invasive public window into a private pedagogical sphere. Surely there is much to be gained from making teaching and learning visible in new ways.

Recommendations for Addressing Evaluation in New Learning Environments

How might evaluation and reward procedures respond in the most positive ways to the consequences of visibility in learning environments while avoiding the negative extension of the kind of surveillance and inhibition that is already, quite frankly, an integral part of the faculty reward structure? To this point, I offer five recommendations for institutions interested in addressing issues of teaching evaluation in new learning environments in the broadest possible contexts:

1. *Link the evaluation of teaching to a context of innovation and inquiry.* One major force in controlling or reversing the negative side of visibility in the teaching evaluation process is for teachers and institutions to continue to develop creative methods of documentation and institutionalized habits of inquiry that enable teachers to be in total control of representing their teaching reflectively and student learning meaningfully. In this sense, the

scholarship of teaching helps reverse the often negative connection between visibility and accountability that has traditionally been the agent of faculty self-policing by turning visibility into an intentional activity, by which faculty make dimensions of their teaching public, asking their own questions about practice and treating teaching as intellectual work. I believe the most important principle for revising teaching evaluation for new learning environments is consonant with the goals of a scholarship of teaching. Submerge teaching evaluation not as part of an accountability process but in a context of innovation, inquiry, and reflection, and as part of this effort make the most effective use of electronic tools and resources for capturing the evidence of learning and the complexities of teaching.

2. *Design evaluation instruments and processes that are attentive to shifting faculty roles, particularly with an emphasis on the complexities of interactivity and the role of faculty as designers and managers of whole learning environments.* One of the major consequences of new faculty roles and new learning environments is the need to design evaluation instruments and processes that respond to these transformations, including course evaluation forms that accommodate pilot courses and student-centered pedagogies and nuanced teaching evaluation procedures (for example, portfolios) that look at courses in the context of development over time and innovations across a curriculum. Also needed are ways of capturing and evaluating the broadest possible range of student learning and learning behaviors, and seeing the role of teachers in the context of designers and managers of whole learning environments (including the design and development of digital materials) and not merely as presenters of information and managers of traditional outcomes.

3. *Distinguish between issues of workload and intellectual work.* With significant shifts in faculty roles, emphasis on interactivity, and whole learning environments come significant changes in faculty workload. Interactive learning in technology-rich environments is tremendously time-consuming in both the creation of the materials and the unfolding of the course. There are, in addition to the significant workload issues, other dimensions of work—intellectual work—that often get conflated with workload issues in the evaluation and reward contexts for faculty doing work with new technologies.

Teaching evaluation procedures must account for the kind of integrative intellectual work that is often involved in effectively producing design learning environments, not just the intellectual work behind the content. Not all on-line or technology-enhanced teaching requires such work. Some on-line teaching through whole course management environments makes use of resources to put traditional pedagogies on-line quickly and uses preestablished communication and collaboration tools to manage student learning. Yet there are many other kinds of environments in which faculty are finding inventive and compelling new ways to present material through digital environments, integrate content and interactivity, and link disciplinary methodology to scaffolded course materials and activities. If teacher evaluation procedures do not reward such work as intellectual work, then we will—again—have the system and results we deserve.[1]

4. *Allow for seeing teaching in new environments in both communal and ecological contexts.* Anyone who has ever worked in a technology-rich environment knows that all successful teaching and learning efforts in new environments are collaborative. Early-adopter faculty also know that it is very difficult to talk about the impact of technology-enhanced pedagogies on learning if those particular pedagogies are relatively anomalous in the curriculum. Some valuation studies on the impact of technology have suggested that it may be impossible to show significant increases in learning (in part due to technology) in a single course, but that impact may be more measurable over time, across the curriculum. Similarly, if one is designing curriculum explicitly for teaching to deepen student understanding (rather than coverage), then the evidence of learning and understanding may be most evident in the transfer of knowledge beyond the course, not in the course itself. The difference here is between questions about "courses" and questions about, as Steve Ehrmann (1997) puts it, "courses of study." Teaching evaluation procedures that accommodate innovation and transformation will try to understand individual courses in communal and ecological contexts. How is the learning in this course like and unlike those around it in the curriculum? How does it meet or diverge from student expectations about traditional learning? How does this course compare to other state-of-the-art courses on other campuses? How is the success of this course circumscribed by the ways that students and faculty make use of available technologies and digital resources (that is, how users interact in the overall ecology of information and technology)? Similarly, faculty work with technology in teaching should be evaluated in the context of institutional (and collective unit) goals for teaching and innovation. Too often institutions articulate goals for technology and education in the curriculum, but departmental evaluations look at each instructor and each course in complete isolation, as if their courses were (in this sense) scholarly publications and the sole responsibility of the individual. Some institutions have moved to offering departmental budget incentives for collective progress in transforming the curriculum in innovative ways. In these contexts, faculty are evaluated in part for their contribution to the department's or unit's teaching goals. This is a relevant and effective strategy irrespective of technology, and especially so given the risk and human overhead involved for faculty engaging in innovative pedagogies in new environments.

5. *Recognize that faculty working in new technology environments are subject to the double bind of equivalence and difference.* It is necessary in the evaluation and reward process to recognize that faculty doing alternative and new work are subject to what we might call the double bind of equivalence and difference. By this I mean that we must consider faculty work in new learning environments both equivalent to the kind of work done in traditional venues (it just *looks* different) *and* that new tools and new envi-

ronments are creating roles, processes, and products that are substantively different from what we have traditionally recognized as teaching. I call it a double bind from my own experience and the experience of many others who have been successful and unsuccessful in the tenure and reward process, trying to make a case for their nontraditional work with new technologies (in teaching and scholarship) and caught many times between the argument that their work should be treated as intrinsically familiar and judged by traditional criteria, on the one hand, and the argument that it is a new kind of work and therefore needs different lenses, if not different standards by which to be judged, on the other. The answer is neither one nor the other but both. And the evaluation of teaching at any given institution must allow for both.

Conclusion

"There are very few traditional paths to tenure, and I did not choose one of them." That was the opening line of my personal statement in my tenure dossier in 1998. In the wake of my tenure case and some press about it, I received dozens of e-mails and had conversations with people all over the world, sharing their similar stories and in many cases confessing their pain, anxiety, and scars over choosing a nontraditional path and its consequences. One of those e-mail exchanges came from a person whose tenure case at a Research I institution had failed. In that process, she wrote, she had lost control of her evidence. Having pointed colleagues to the visible on-line environment in which her basic writing students were doing their work, in at least one instance, selections of student papers, out of context, were being printed off and brought into the process as questionable examples of student learning. Wanting only to judge her teaching by traditional standards and disallowing that a different kind of learning process might require different ways of judging, her colleagues were (ironically) also willing to take work that was newly accessible and visible through new approaches out of the context that made those approaches comprehensible and defensible.

All such cases are complex, and it is not appropriate to give more details. But one message is clear: there are both promise and peril in the new visibility. If we are to avoid penalizing the innovators, as well as avoid foreclosing the possibilities of new technology environments to change (for the better) what we think of as teaching and learning, then we must put these new visibilities and possibilities in the broadest, most open-minded evaluative context.

Note

1. For an example of an evaluation policy statement that attempts to focus on intellectual work across traditional evaluation categories, see the 1996 report of the Modern Language Associations Commission on Professional Service, *Making Faculty Work Visible: Reinterpreting Professional Service, Teaching, and Research in the Fields of Language and Literature.*

References

Bass, R. *American Literary Traditions: A Hypertext Course Portfolio.* Georgetown University, 1998. [http://www.georgetown.edu/bassr/portfolio/amlit/]

Ehrmann, S. C. "Asking the Right Questions: What Does Research Tell Us About Technology and Higher Learning." *Change,* 1997, 27, 20–27. [http://www.learner.org/edtech/rscheval/rightquestion.html]

Flashlight Program: Helping You Analyze and Improve Educational Uses of Technology. TLT Group, with the American Association for Higher Education, 1998. [http://www.tltgroup.org/programs/flashlight.html]

Hutchings, P. (ed.). *Making Teaching Community Property: A Menu for Peer Collaboration and Peer Review.* Washington, D.C.: AAHE, 1996.

Hutchings, P. (ed.). *The Course Portfolio: How Faculty Can Examine Their Teaching to Advance Practice and Improve Student Learning.* Washington, D.C.: American Association for Higher Education, 1998.

Lieberman, D. "Evaluating Teaching Through Electronic Classroom Assessment." In P. Seldin and others (eds.), *Changing Practices in Evaluating Teaching: A Practical Guide to Improved Faculty Performance and Promotion/Tenure Decisions.* Bolton, Mass.: Anker Publishing, 1999.

Modern Language Association. Commission on Faculty Service. *Making Faculty Work Visible: Reinterpreting Professional Service, Teaching, and Research in the Fields of Language and Literature.* New York: Modern Language Association, 1996.

Noble, D. F. "Digital Diploma Mill: The Automation of Higher Education." *First Monday,* 1998, 3.

North, J. D. "Administrative Courage to Evaluate the Complexities of Teaching." In P. Seldin and others (eds.), *Changing Practices in Evaluating Teaching: A Practical Guide to Improved Faculty Performance and Promotion/Tenure Decisions.* Bolton, Mass.: Anker Publishing, 1999.

Seldin, P., and others. *Changing Practices in Evaluating Teaching: A Practical Guide to Improved Faculty Performance and Promotion/Tenure Decisions.* Bolton, Mass.: Anker Publishing, 1999.

Shulman, L. S. "Course Anatomy." In P. Hutchings (ed.), *The Course Portfolio: How Faculty Can Examine Their Teaching to Advance Practice and Improve Student Learning.* Washington, D.C.: American Association for Higher Education, 1998.

Shulman, L. S. "Taking Learning Seriously." *Change,* Sept.–Oct. 1999.

Syverson, M. A. *The On-line Learning Record.* University of Texas, 2000. [http://www.cwrl.utexas.edu/~syverson/olr/]

Virtual Geography Department. University of Texas, 1999. [http://www.utexas.edu/depts/grg/virtdept/contents.html]

World Lecture Hall. University of Texas, 1998. [http://www.utexas.edu/world/lecture/]

RANDALL J. BASS is associate professor of English and executive director of the Center for New Designs in Learning and Scholarship at Georgetown University.

5

To consider the actual complexity of teaching, to consider its several contexts, checklists and surveys are insufficient.

Situational Evaluation of Teaching on Campus

Robert E. Stake, Edith J. Cisneros-Cohernour

The current state of the art of formal evaluation of college teaching is simplistic and inconsequential. Faculty work is a complex enterprise, but most assessment procedures are insensitive to its broad responsibility and situationality. An effective evaluation of teaching requires the study of institutional goals, classroom environments, administrative organization and operations, curricular content, student achievement, and the impact of programs on state and society (Shulman, 1986; Cave, Hanney, Kogan, and Travett, 1988). Teaching can be judged properly only in the context of these other factors, and if no effort is made to study them, the evaluation of teaching probably will be invalid.

We support multiple evaluative efforts. Thus, we deemphasize instructor traits and styles and even student outcomes, and instead emphasize instructor duties, calling for personal judgment of the evaluator, and urging consideration of the instructor as a member of a faculty team. Finally, we oppose using evaluation to standardize campus teaching.

Hazards

Many professors (as with people in all other kinds of work) consider evaluation a threat, and with reason. Whether the evaluation is valid or invalid, they may get hurt. The evaluation will inevitably be less sensitive to their aims and talents than anyone would like. It will be more attuned to campus institutional aims and structures (Meyer, Scott, and Deal, 1981), and to those quite imperfectly. More insidious, evaluation sometimes is used to harass or censor. What a professor has to say should not go unevaluated, but

NEW DIRECTIONS FOR TEACHING AND LEARNING, no. 83, Fall 2000   © Jossey-Bass, a Wiley company

action based on evaluation should not violate academic freedom.[1] Only when it can be demonstrated that the capacity for education will be helped more than hurt by the formal processes of teacher evaluation should they occur. The burden of demonstration rests with administrators. It should be a stern obligation. The harmony and respect of the faculty, and thus the quality of classroom learning environments, should not be put at risk just because evaluation of teaching might make some things better.

Instructor evaluation—the appraisal of qualifications and performance of the individual college teacher—has at least four purposes:

- To provide data for the reward of merit and the correction of shortcoming
- To aid selection of the best-qualified persons for new assignments and retention of the most needed in old
- To assist in continuing professional education for professors
- To contribute to the understanding of the operation of the department and college as a whole

Although these purposes regularly coexist, they get in each other's way. Data for one purpose may unethically be used for another purpose; for example, data volunteered for staff improvement may wrongly be used for accountability. The purposes, contexts, techniques, and consequences need to be seen as a systemic whole if the evaluation is to be validated and beneficial.

Uniqueness and Comparability

In one of the classics of personnel evaluation, Lee Cronbach and Goldine Gleser (1965) made an important distinction between *placement* and *selection*. If we are evaluating someone who is already a faculty member with the expectation of remaining so, we will call it a placement situation. From the evaluation we hope to get a better idea of talents and shortcomings. Noting both, we want to consider modification of the teaching situation that will improve working conditions and performance—usually a minor adjustment, but sometimes a major one.

For placement evaluation, one concentrates on the responsibilities of instruction and the immediate work context. For selection, that is, selecting one of many candidates for a position, immediate circumstances are not so important. In most of the following, the discussion will be on the placement situation.

One of the greater mistakes in teacher evaluation procedure is to concentrate on comparisons with faculty members en masse. Standards on which action is based will shift under different circumstances, according to different reference groups, and as the purposes of evaluation change. But reference should primarily be made to the unique situation of the instructor being evaluated. There are three reference scales (each running, say, from bad teaching to superb) to keep in mind: (1) the quality of this teaching (as certain people perceive it to be—without immediate reference to other professors), (2) how good this teaching *might be* (for this instructor) in this setting, and (3) how well other instructors teach (locally or wherever else). For improving the teaching of faculty members already hired and not easily reassigned, extra attention needs to be paid to scale 2, the range between the best and the worst each instructor could be given the conditions of work here, especially the conditions that can be little altered by the faculty. It tells us of room to improve and something of effort made to be *this* good. The range of "worst possible" to "best possible" (within a context) cannot be stated precisely, but even roughly conceived, is needed for appraisal leading to staff development and program improvement.

There is no one ideal teacher. Even in the narrowest training program, students have many things to learn. However standardized the pedagogical plan, different instructors teach different things. For example, the instructor who emphasizes critical thinking seldom models mobilization for action. The need for diverse talents is not because good teachers do not teach broadly, but because teachers are consistent in the kinds of learning situations they create. Dissimilar teachers create a useful range of learning situations.

Professors, even teaching assistants, have considerable autonomy in the classroom yet regularly act in concert. It should be obvious, then, that evaluating one person's teaching depends on recognizing what talents are already available among other members of the faculty. In other words, one needs to evaluate not only individual instructors but teams of teaching faculty too.

Effective teaching requires an understanding of what else is being taught by others right now, as well as what has been taught and what is still to come. It requires an understanding of topics and a good order of presentation. An evaluation of individual instructors is not complete without taking into account how the teacher works with others of the faculty and the strengths and weaknesses of those people. Every teacher is a member of one or several groups, and each group has its own uniqueness and context.

Criteria

Evaluation is usually thought of as based on criteria, with certain descriptive scores indicating more or less of something and drawing forth a judgment of goodness or badness. Whether the judgment follows or precedes explication of the criterion is not always clear, but criteria usually can be found when anything is evaluated. The criteria by which teaching faculties are evaluated are numerous (see Dunkin and Biddle, 1974, for example).

Exhaustive as the lists may be, no one set of criteria can adequately fit most teaching situations. Furthermore, high marks on all criteria do not indicate the most valuable instructor for all situations. And an excess of any good quality can be too much of a good thing.[2] The ways to wrong are many. For something beyond a superficial indication of the quality of teaching, we at least need information of diverse types, relating to diverse situations, and drawn from diverse sources.

Common to many formal appraisals of teaching are checklists featuring criteria such as knowledge of subject matter, effectiveness of student control, and quality of lesson plans (Braskamp and Ory, 1994). Such characteristics are often not highly correlated with effective teaching, but they serve to announce what authorities admire in instructors. Such checklists are accepted as legitimate by most faculty members, particularly when objective-appearing procedures are needed to gain promotion or protect the status quo.

There are rules for the sensible use of checklists. For example, sums or averages (across items or across instructors) are seldom meaningful. Such aggregates have seldom been validated empirically. Even when used properly, evaluative checklists usually produce nothing more refined than impressions. Most are deliberately context free, and that often leads to unwarranted generalization. Understanding the qualification of instructors requires review of what they have done in especially sensitive situations. Gathering good data on those situations is difficult, but should not be avoided. Just because it happened only once is not a proper basis for ignoring a critical act.

No group providing evaluative observations is likely to agree unanimously on criteria and standards. When asked to evaluate an instructor, students tend to emphasize general personality characteristics; peer faculty members tend to emphasize camaraderie; administrators admire compliance.[3] Within groups, of course, there are differences as well. These views should not be expected to converge. There is no one correct view of the quality of teaching. The purpose of evaluation should not be to get a single rating or descriptor (Doyle, 1982) but to learn the faceted quality of teaching, partly as perceived by people who have a stake in it.

Administrative Evaluation

Management of teaching cannot be effective without some assessment of teaching competence. The best and the worst we have is informal faculty evaluation—administrator driven, sometimes capricious, and sometimes more aimed at minimizing embarrassment than optimizing service to students. Administrative evaluation most often is informal review, such as that of a department head's intuitively valuing an instructor, but surfacing into formality when something goes wrong, when promotion or an increment of pay depends on it, or when a teaching award is in the offing.

Feldman (1989) observed that administrators seem to base their evaluation on the reputation of the faculty member and participation in departmental activities, such as committee service. Often when administrators evaluate professors, they play the roles of both judge and coach—a combination that seldom serves both evaluation and professional development well (Genova, Madoff, Chink, and Thomas, 1976).

The real problem is not subjectivity. Intuition works surprisingly well. Professors highly esteemed tend to be sensitive to what students are doing. Administrators overemphasize evidence of student satisfaction, but many have a good idea of which classrooms are good for career development. Most students are in some ways personally helped. But few who are incompetent at teaching are dismissed, or helped to get better, or even officially recognized. The instructors themselves have reservations about current administrative reviews, but they tremble at the thought that the coming "rigorous system" will be simplistic and punitive.

An increasing number of administrators are caught up in a technical form of campus management that promises measurement of teaching effectiveness, sometimes indicating that the worth of teaching can be indicated in the value added to student careers. The usual suggestion is that student achievement or performance tests will be devised that show gain in targeted knowledge and skill. There are three huge defects in this campaign: almost all the important learning for course and career ladder cannot be measured with the current level of testing,[4] only a few of any gains discerned could be attributed to a particular instructor, and the pressure for measurable performance waters down the curriculum. At the same time that campus administrations become more business oriented and inventive of spreadsheets, the uncertainty of markets, methods, and staffing grows. Only a few of the most professional and learned fields are so unchanging that one can indicate with confidence what knowledge and skill will be critical in tomorrow's world. Those uncertainties do not call for instructors to ignore preparation of the coming generation, but the grounds for evaluating teaching effectiveness by standardized testing are not being found.

Teacher Traits

Most administrators who move to formal evaluating rely heavily on checklists and scales. Some do the occasional in-class observation. The personnel evaluation literature and organization development literature provide an abundance of criteria. In the open-ended sections of rating instruments, special merit is to be described.[5]

The literature is well endowed with observation forms such as the classic bipolar list of attributes from David Ryans (1960), shown in Exhibit 5.1. Here an instructor can be marked as "partial" or "fair," "autocratic" or "democratic," "aloof" or "responsive," "restricted" or "understanding," and so on. These are personality characteristics. But good teachers are found of any personality orientation, and too much of any kind in a department is problematic. Such traits are useful for discussions of teaching, but they are not at the heart of good faculty evaluation.

Exhibit 5.1. An Example of Bipolar Traits Descriptive of Teachers

Partial . . . Fair
Autocratic . . . Democratic
Aloof . . . Responsive
Restricted . . . Understanding
Harsh . . . Kindly
Dull . . . Stimulating
Stereotyped . . . Original
Apathetic . . . Alert
Unimpressive . . . Attractive
Evading . . . Responsible
Erratic . . . Steady
Excitable . . . Poised
Uncertain . . . Confident
Inflexible . . . Adaptable
Pessimistic . . . Optimistic
Immature . . . Integrated
Narrow . . . Broad

Source: Adapted from Ryans (1960, p. 86). Used with permission.

Teaching Styles

More related to the quality of teaching than instructor traits are the instructor's teaching styles. When we put forward models of good teaching, we describe in some detail the pedagogical approach (Broudy, 1963). Each of us draws from previous experience and finds much to agree with in terms of what is satisfying and what is offensive teaching behavior. Style does have a lot to do with improving teaching quality. The suggestions in Exhibit 5.2 were drawn from a book of advice to faculty members on our campus made by the Office of Instructional Resources (1983), a group evaluating teaching and supporting teacher improvement.

These teacher behaviors constitute good advice. Many of them have been studied and found to be correlated both statistically and experientially with effective teaching. But they should not be used as standardized evaluation. Were they to be included in formal evaluation of teaching, they would violate the rights of the faculty member.

This issue is not easy to understand, but it is certain that evaluation must not be based on statistical correlation alone between teacher traits or teacher behaviors and well-measured teaching effectiveness. As long as there is less than perfect correlation, it is wrong to penalize an effective instructor because his or her style is unconventional (Scriven, 1988). The research might, for example, show strong links between showing respect for students and the amount students learn—but as long as respecting students has not been explicitly defined as a teaching obligation, then the teacher is free to give or withhold respect. Evaluation cannot be based on how effective at teaching we would predict instructors would be. Our obligation is to base the evaluation on how effective they are.

Exhibit 5.2. Suggestions for Delivering an Effective Lecture

- Always try to start and end on time.
- Start with a sense of authority, with your voice louder than usual. This will assist you in gaining their attention.
- Be sure that your voice can be heard, and your writing is readable, by all of your students. Have your students, a colleague, or TA give you feedback in this regard.
- The more formal the lecture and the larger your student enrollment, so also should your gestures, word emphasis, slowing of pace, and use of silent pauses be more intensified and deliberate.
- When using visual aids, be sure:
  —Your print is large enough for back row visibility
  —Your pace is slow enough so that your students can read or copy content
  —Continually maintain direct eye contact with students in all sections of the room.
- Plan for more content in the event that you are done much sooner than you expected.
- Your visuals should augment your lecturing, not BE the lecture. Phrases rather than complete sentences should be used on the visuals. When definitions are necessary, provide handouts or slowly write or read the definition while repeating.
- Record your voice or videotape yourself as you lecture so that you can listen for pitch variation, pacing, volume, enunciation, pronunciation, general comprehensibility, eye contact, gesturing, and distracting movement.
- Schedule a time to be videotaped (consult IMS) as you lecture and have an IMS specialist consult with you during a playback viewing.

Source: Office of Instructional Resources (1989, p. 27). Used by permission.

Duties of Instruction

College administrators get good mileage out of student ratings obtained from checklists or questionnaires describing teacher behaviors, outcomes, and duties. Rating systems have been developed to an art and need to be part of any comprehensive evaluation of teaching.[6] In ordinary classroom use, however, they cannot be treated as a representative sample of student population, even for one classroom, but as an important communication from the students who respond. One can learn as much from so-called deviant respondents as from the modal. Standardized checklists and questionnaires can be useful, but it should be noticed that few of them are concentrated on duties, partly because students have little opportunity for observing many of the duties identified below.

What professors are obligated as teachers to do, in and out of class, needs to be at the center of the evaluation (Scriven, 1974; Borich, 1977). But what they are obligated to do is not set forth in contract or by law or edict. When failing to win tenure or promotion, the professor is charged with insensitivity, ethical violation, or failing to complete work but not a violation of an explicit duty. Yet it is just such sense of duty, as beheld by administrators, colleagues, and students, as well as self, that is the first basis for formally evaluating quality of instruction. In this sense, it is common to find lists of duties used to assess an instructor performance. For faculty evaluation, Michael Scriven (1988a, 1988b) developed an approach called

Duties-Based Teacher Evaluation (DBTE).[7] The duties of the instructor according to this definition are set out in Exhibit 5.3.

An important distinction should be made between what can be considered generic duty and being a good department member. Both are grounds for evaluation, and both are negotiable, but one is an implicit contract, and the other is some form of experiential understanding with administrators and fellow members. When discussing responsibilities and advancement with a professor, it is not uncommon for administrators to identify needs and expectations, such as attending faculty meetings, turning in grades and other forms on time, avoiding grade inflation, fulfilling office hours, and so on. Such are the things that instructors should do, but without broad and explicit endorsement across the campus, most are not duties. Many are pressures for compliance and teamwork, not even correlates of good teaching and certainly not duties. We will mention again the need for diversity within any faculty. Too much compliance is a bad thing, though what administrator would ever testify having had it?

Institutionalizing such a list of duties can lead to undesirable consequences.[8] If a duties list becomes part of contract or regulation, it can become a barrier to the development of new and creative forms of instruction. It can lead administrators and committees to put more emphasis on the rubric than on the instruction being evaluated. Here too, the search for objectivity may lead not only to construct invalidity but to consequential invalidity[9] as well.

In DBTE, Scriven urges us to be explicit about the duties commonly shared among faculty members and to treat them in a quantitative and comparative manner. His primary reason is to reduce bias. When language is clear and agreed on, the chances are lower that evaluator bias will determine the outcomes. Bias does need control. But often it is not possible to distinguish between bias and deep understanding. Concentrating on clear and precise wording diminishes attention to certain complex relationships that may move the recognition of merit and worth in a different direction. In the following section, we urge more attention to disciplining complex judgments of teaching value and less attention to representation of merit on scalar dimensions.

A Judgmental Alternative

The duties-based teacher evaluation approach addresses the central issue in the evaluation of college teaching: the definition of what constitutes good instruction. Scriven (1994) defines it in terms of duties: "Good teaching is whatever scores well on the duties list" (p. 33). Although this approach moves away from narrow outcomes-based teacher evaluation and focuses on what instructors must do, it has limitations similar to those using outcome indicators, teacher traits, and teaching styles: it does not aggressively represent good teaching.

If we understand broadly and deeply what instructors do, we will avoid relying alone on criterion-based evaluations built up from generalization of

Exhibit 5.3. Professional Duties of an Instructor

1. Knowledge of duties	Includes knowledge of the law and regulations applying to their college or institution as well as the expectations at a particular school. It includes understanding of the curriculum requirements and duties. Includes understanding that the obligation to follow orders and regulations must be given significant weight; but that it never constitutes an excuse for seriously unprofessional or ethical standards.
2. Knowledge of school and community	Includes an understanding of any special characteristics, background, or ideology of the school, its staff and students, and its environment.
3. Knowledge of subject matter	Includes knowledge (a) in the field(s) of special competence; (b) in across-the-curriculum subjects like English, study skills, personal/vocational awareness, computer studies, and so forth.
4. Instructional design	Includes (a) course design, (b) selection and creation of materials, (c) competent use of available resources, (d) course and curriculum evaluation, (e) knowledge and procedures for addressing the needs of special groups, (f) use of human resources (for example, curriculum specialists, audiovisual and methods specialists) when appropriate.
5. Gathering information about student learning	Includes (a) testing skills, (b) grading knowledge (marking, scoring, rating, diagnosing), (c) establishing grading procedures, (d) grade allocation.
6. Providing information about student learning	Includes (a) to each student, (b) on each test, (c) to the administration, (d) to parents, guardians, and other appropriate authorities.
7. Classroom skills	Includes (a) communication skills, (b) management skills under standard (for example, discipline, achievement covering the designed content with the appropriate level of student understanding), and emergency conditions (for example, fire, flood, tornado/typhoon, earthquake, volcanic eruption, blizzard, and so forth).
8. Personal characteristics	Includes professional attitude and engagement on professional development (for example, engaging in systematic improvement of class materials and plans, procedures for self-evaluation and development when appropriate).
9. Service to the profession	Includes (a) knowledge about professional issues, (b) knowledge and performance in accordance with professional ethics, (c) helping beginners and peers, (d) work on projects for other professionals, and (e) contributions to the research from which the profession draws its skills and expertise.

Note: Scriven treats each category of data as a dimension or a criterion that defines an instructor's job. He developed the list by conducting a review of numerous official documents that was later presented to experienced teachers in the United States, Canada, and Australia for their reaction and suggestions to the items of the list.

Source: Adapted from Scriven (1994, pp. 25–32). Used by permission.

performance. Part of our thinking of teaching quality will draw on a holistic appreciation of individual teaching moments. We need both intuition and logical reasoning to identify merit. Within the holistic view, merit in the instructor's teaching is situational and complex beyond specification. A certain performance of teaching duty "is good for some student needs some of the time, better and poorer at other times." (See the parallel to interpretive program evaluation in Stake and others, 1997, p. 97.)

In DBTE, good teaching is defined primarily in terms of instructor performance in meeting the duties list. We appreciate this contribution, yet believe that an instructor's teaching is complex beyond duties representation and resists any one simplex of values. Goodness of teaching is situational; it can be different for different purposes, different students and contexts, and different times. Having a list of duties as a criterion for evaluating teaching presents the advantage of bringing aspects that have been overlooked and sources of evidence that have been ignored (Scriven, 1995, p. 36). It should be perceived as a useful and practical component, but one that seldom will represent enough of the complexities of instruction. Merging the criterial values with a deliberated holistic view of teaching quality is the responsibility of the evaluator (administrator, mentor, or committee).

Scriven's (1995) approach is of special interest because it attempts "to reduce the judgmental elements of the evaluation by introducing . . . objective criteria" (p. 121). He sees judgment as problematic and claims that evaluations generally improve with the reduction of bias. He acknowledges that no human contemplation can be completely bias free but that good evaluation manages to hold judgment to a minimum.

Scriven urges diminishing bias by explicit definitions of duties and using mathematical weighting to arrive at a final nonjudgmental synthesis of value. But judgment and bias too are undifferentiated parts of any good evaluation effort. There is bias not only from each of the main data sources used in the evaluation of college teaching but also bias in the design and conduct of the evaluation. Even if we had the most comprehensive list of duties, and one that instructors might agree on, evaluator bias still operates.

Bias is not just imprecision. Some bias is discrimination. Bias against a certain teaching style or cultural orientation is discrimination, hurtful to the instructor, and hurtful to his or her students. It remains a serious problem in departments. The real and immediate danger of hurtful bias cannot be sufficiently derived from codes of ethics, regulations, or standards, and it cannot be avoided by precise definitions of duties. It helps to have reference documents, but the complexity of actual situations also requires human perception, dialogue, interpretation, and personal judgment.

Forty years of research on faculty evaluation has been biased toward simplicity, management efficiency, and ease of communication.[10] Much of it has tried to reduce valuing to a formal rubric (Mabry, 1999; Berlak and others, 1992). It is as if we should forgo the validity of the evaluation in our honoring of objectivity. By putting primary attention on precise and standardized wording, we can expect to diminish attention on how the instructor has performed in critical moments and particular circumstances. Culturally rich interpretations are biased, but they are essential to the understanding of the value of education. Evaluation without such interpretation is simplistic, reduced to what can be defined and quantified. Bias itself is not the essence of the problem of valid faculty evaluations.

We feel uncomfortable with simple scales and notions of causal links.[11] Intuition and conscious reasoning should not be overrun by ratings, indicators, characteristics, or lists of duties. Evaluation of teaching requires personal interpretation and judgment—not necessarily in place of criteria, categories and indicators but, especially, after them. Judgment should be the pinnacle of the evaluation. Rather than put final effort into refining dimensions, we think that more effort should be put into improving judgment. All practicing evaluators should seek understanding about the particular teaching by studying it from different points of view and frames of reference, by submitting it to challenge and review. In this way, the complex merits of teaching will not be lost in a simple indicator. Rather, context-relevant discussion of multiple meanings of quality is made possible. Through dialectic critique, we can improve intuition, quality recognition, and judgment (Stake and others, 1997).

Individual and Collective Accountability

The evaluation of teaching needs to address the issue of accountability. A professor, as a teacher, is accountable to many people: students, fellow instructors, administrators, citizens, herself or himself. Instructors make agreements, explicit or implicit, with these people. They are accountable for what they do and for what those other people understand they are doing.

The instructor is responsible for many duties, having agreed explicitly by signing a contract and writing a course description, more indirectly by assigning projects and authoring examinations. Through pedagogical behavior, without words spoken or written, he or she assumes many additional responsibilities. By using a textbook (unless disaffirming it), she or he agrees to teach its subject matter. By giving sympathy and consolation, he or she agrees to attend to the needs of aspirants to career lines. When an instructor is suddenly inconsistent, he or she is not accountable to those who have developed learning expectations from an accustomed behavior.

Accountability, first of all, is a matter of doing what has been promised. Some of the promises are collegewide. The whole department is accountable—accountable not only for student learning but for much more: personal safety in the building, introduction to different ethnic values, opportunity to relate to different professional role models, and egalitarian distribution of learning opportunities. And each instructor shares in the responsibility.

A second aspect of accountability is identification of one's responsibility. Programs, course descriptions, and syllabi spell out teaching responsibilities, but each instructor refines the identification. Professors are not being accountable if they fail to help people realize the nature of the college's responsibility. President Truman displayed a motto on his desk: "The buck stops here." The accountable instructor is not one who passes the buck, not one who gives irate students the runaround, but one who helps the department staff allocate and discharge their responsibility.

Instructors have an obligation to let people know what they are doing. This is a third feature of teaching accountability: disclosure. Disclosure of action goes beyond identification of intention. The instructor has an obligation to facilitate review—whether professional, student, or public review—of what he or she is doing. Accountability, besides being a fulfillment of one's promises and the identification of personal responsibility, is a matter of disclosure. Even though much teacher-student interaction should occur in an atmosphere of privacy, with provision for the rights of both student and teacher, improprieties are not protected, and what in essence and in general is happening is not a private matter.

This three-dimensional definition of accountability does not require that a instructor determine and disclose the impact of his or her teaching. Instructors are not responsible for presenting data on student performance unless they have explicitly or implicitly agreed to do so. Graded papers, conferences with parents, and student examination data are questionable indicators of teaching effectiveness. On most campuses, except for those in probationary status, instructors are not obligated to submit student performance data to anyone but students. Most teaching today can be considered accountable without presenting criterial evidence to administrators. Given the limited relationship between student test performance and teaching quality (Stake, 1995), that omission is quite defensible. Nevertheless, when departmental examination has officially been defined as a component of accountability, instructors have the obligation to comply. In most cases, most instructors work hand in hand with their supervisors and are, in fact, making an effort to describe how well their students are doing on tests, how much they are increasing understandings, and whether the more advanced students are doing well in career preparation.

It is too easy to think that accountability might be satisfied by having acceptable test scores. Accountability is a matter of fulfilling agreements. In some places, that includes keeping test scores above a certain level, but in most good places, it does not. An instructor is most accountable to people close at hand. What those people and the instructor perceive the teaching responsibility to be is the primary content of teacher accountability.

Community of Practice

The traditional concept of evaluating college teaching involves the evaluation of each individual autonomous instructor in each classroom across the campus. This approach sees the teaching and its evaluation only as taking place in the classroom and as a single instructor's responsibility.[12]

Here we address a competing concept that focuses on evaluating the contribution each instructor makes to the maintenance and improvement of all instructional programs in the department. What instructors do directly for students in their classes is, of course, important, but what they contribute to the integrity of all department offerings is important too. A charismatic lecturer or innovative lab organizer or personalistic mentor may contribute little to the upgrade of weak, misdirected, frivolous, and outdated courses in the department. Both individual and team contributions need to be considered if campus teaching is to be adequately evaluated (Porter, 1989).

Collaboration across a department faculty about matters of teaching is not new but remains peripheral. Writing about a faculty as a "community of practice"[13] has become identified with Philip Morrison and John Seely Brown and colleagues at the Institute for Research on Learning at Menlo Park.[14] These writers (Wenger, 1991; Brown, 1997; Alpert, 1998) have noted the scarcity of campus departments where instructors work closely together to maintain and improve teaching programs.[15] Wenger said, "Even those who speak about learning organizations, life long learning, or the information society do so mostly in terms of individual learners and information processes. The notion of communities of practice helps us break this mold" (p. 7).

Standard practice in many departments on many campuses is for individual professors to offer advanced courses that reflect their own scholarly distinctions and for graduate students and instructors primarily interested in becoming research professors to teach the prerequisites. These departments are a collection of stars and lesser lights, experts and novices, iconoclasts, professors worrying not very much about department offering as a whole, seldom even talking among themselves about educational issues. A community of teaching practice, it is not.

Daniel Alpert (1998) has written cogently about the drain on department vigor to have the National Science Foundation and philanthropic groups finance researchers and scholars more or less directly to the individual principal investigator.[16] The same problem appears to exist in thinking of teaching as an individual responsibility rather than departmental.

Teaching brilliantly or pitifully, and collaborating well or poorly in instruction, both individuals and departments need to be taken into account in evaluating campus teaching. A system that looks only at the ongoing classroom and ignores the scrutiny and problem solving of curriculum development is an impoverished effort to evaluate college teaching.

Wheeler Loomis, once head of the Physics Department on our campus, used to keep a list of faculty names in his pocket, a list of "those who contributed most to the department."[17] His ratings of instructors might have neglected eye contact, fair grading, and classroom charm, but it recognized teaching as a collective responsibility.

Let us mention some common problems with campus instruction:

- Instructors have poor communication habits.
- Organized assistance for individuals is almost nonexistent.
- Articulation between adjacent and subsequent courses is weak.
- Course difficulty is set to screen candidates for advanced work rather than to teach each student as much as possible.

The last two of these problems are not prominent in students' evaluation of instruction because students have little knowledge of the content and ongoing evolution of a discipline. And many faculty members are so specialized they do not know what is happening in other corners of the department or in allied disciplines. Articulation and course difficulty are problems for a faculty as a whole, yet many instructors can get good ratings for teaching even while ignoring them.

All four of the problems call for collective attention of a faculty. The quality of an individual faculty member to campus teaching should be partly based on his or her contributions to the remedy of such problems.

Case Study

We would like to describe a senior professor Edith was studying.[18] He recognized himself and his department chair recognized that he had picked up more than his share of student complaints. We will talk about him here in terms of the mobilization of his faculty colleagues to increase the effectiveness of teaching.

> George Alderman, a senior professor in practical sciences, was receiving low to moderate student ratings. He had taught in his department more than twenty years and recently was teaching a mathematics-related course required of all students in the department.
>
> In former years, George taught the same class each term to all who enrolled. The students gave him and the course low ratings. Then the department head divided the students among three instructors, each of whom then taught two classes, with forty-five students each, meeting twice a week. After one semester, one of the instructors obtained high ratings for his teaching; George and the other got low ratings. George sought help from the Division of Instructional Development. His peers chose to work together.
>
> A semester later, only George was rated low. His ratings actually went down, partly because he called for student teamwork and with each student grading each other's participation. One of George's students formally charged him with "capricious grading." The department head sent George a letter asking him to find a way to improve.[19] In interviews, the head spoke of the need for improvement of teaching but acknowledged she was not providing faculty members with other feedback on instruction or creating mechanisms to support teaching.

George's colleague Professor Edwards said, "Student ratings are not measuring teaching effectiveness. I advocate use of classroom visitations by peer faculty. Not only would this increase the rate at which junior professors improve their teaching skills, but we would have more reliable feedback regarding teaching effectiveness. However, classroom observations are quite time-consuming. Since teaching is not rewarded to the extent that research is, many faculty members feel that it is not in their best interest to do this."

George's department head agreed: "We would like to use various sources such as alumni or peers to evaluate instruction in addition to current students but this is not possible. We use students because they are accessible."

George commented on the help from the instructional specialist: "I consider her the only source of meaningful feedback that I have to improve my teaching."

In other words, there was no community of practice to help George decide how he should teach. George and his colleagues allowed that peers could be a valuable source of feedback, but they stuck to the idea that help should be person to person rather than collective.

George's colleague Bill Wilson said, "On at least four occasions I have asked a colleague to sit in my class and provide me with feedback. Sometimes the feedback from a peer is productive; sometimes it is not. My experience is that the feedback from a peer is more useful when it is provided in private— if your department does not know the information."

Another colleague, Frank Edwards, said, "In this department, a formal mentoring program does not exist. It is quite common, however, for informal mentoring, where one faculty member helps another, to take place."

And George said, "The feedback from a colleague may work if several professors teach the same subject, they observe each other's classes, and then they have an informal conversation. But this needs to be provided as consultation, not with professors writing reports for the administration."

George's case provides an example of a department that has expressly communicated its intentions for improving teaching. But no support is provided at the department level, so George and other instructors are left on their own. Most of them looked for feedback. Their efforts to improve teaching did not include a discussion of the responsibility of each professor to help others improve. This was seen to be an individual responsibility of the instructor.

In spite of the fact that George's department was not accustomed to thinking of teaching by a community of practice, it was clear that some colleagueship was available to assist him. It is the responsibility of department and campus leaders to change the perspective away from the star system (in both research and teaching) to a collaborative enterprise.

The Goal Context

Evaluation of teaching, as with evaluation of other aspects of the educational system, needs evaluators who can analyze goals. Every department has patrons and clients to whom it has commitments. It is the responsibility of administrators to interpret the wishes of the community and the needs of students, and thus to shape a formal curricular plan.[20]

Administrators have the responsibility to formalize department goals, particularly long-range curricular goals. In words or in action, attendant to ideology and social mission, individual instructors set intermediate and tactical goals. Within constraints of custom and taste, classroom instructors choose strategies and tactics. The integrity of a curricular program is maintained only when faculty members perceive themselves—within limits and a certain division of labor—to be free to pursue department goals as each sees fit (see Peters and Waterman, 1984). Supervisors or committees charged with evaluative responsibility should assess the discharge of such responsibility but should not presume that there is but one proper way of teaching or that there is but one set of educational objectives, even for a single lesson. They may make known to the instructor certain perceptions and valuation of past contributions and certain hopes for the future, but based on what we know about teaching, the final choice of intermediate goals and means of instruction should largely be left to the one who teaches.

Maintaining meritorious teaching is one of the primary responsibilities of the administrative staff. The administrators should collect evidence of merit—or lack of it—from various sources. They should give some small attention to results of achievement testing and should at least informally follow up former students. Throughout the year and across the years, they should encourage each faculty member formally and informally to submit evidence of teaching merit. Together they should submit plans and artifacts of teaching to the scrutiny of experts in subject matter and pedagogy.

Each person who teaches is responsible for contributing to the evidence of teaching effectiveness. The evidence may be process or product data, and preferably both. Process data (such as lesson plans, counsel, and self-evaluation) are useful because we believe that certain teaching activities promote student accomplishment (Marton and Säljö, 1976). For example, it is expected that a conspicuous concern for ethical behavior in the classroom will encourage ethical behavior in youth. Product data provide actual observation of accomplishment or correlates of accomplishment (for example, achievement tests indirectly indicate whether students understand certain important relationships). Product data at first appear preferable, but the need for assessing the quality of working conditions and the difficulty of attributing student achievement to what the instructor does make inclusion of process data a necessity.

Leaving Teachers in Charge

Because autonomy is not only a fact of life but a demonstrated contribution to good work, the means available to administrators for redirecting instructional programs are and should be limited.[21] In many places, merit pay is not offered, and modification of assignment is greatly constrained. Still admin-

istrators can modify the direction of teaching through persuasion, reallocation of incidental resources and class load, reassignment of responsibility, and
sometimes employment of aides or even additional faculty members.

Professors themselves are mainly responsible for the continuing
improvement of instruction. Administrators are responsible for encouraging
and facilitating that improvement. The following should be provided by
campus services for voluntary, sometimes confidential, use:

Checklists of classroom, laboratory, and field conditions that have been
    demonstrated to promote learning
Course content reviews (selections of topics, texts, resource works, and so
    forth) conducted outside the classroom by experienced peers and spe-
    cially trained supervisors
Observational and remediation services by specialists in instruction and
    testing

Feedback from these three sources will work best in the long run if seen (as
it should be) as the property of the individual instructor, not to be reviewed
by others without his or her release.

The worth of an educational program is not entirely but is at least
partly attributable to its impact on students. Impacts are difficult to measure. Part of the evaluation of teaching should be an attempt to assess student learning. Some indication of gain in skill, understanding, and attitude
can be obtained informally, but also formally through disciplined observation and performance tests, and to a lesser extent with achievement tests
and interest and attitude inventories. These measures should be seen as
merely sampling a full set of achievements.

Conclusion

We have discussed the evaluation of teaching with an emphasis on the context of work, the multidimensionality of competence, and the uniqueness
of individual faculty members. These qualities, plus emphasis on personal
intentionality and empathic understanding, have been common aspects of
naturalistic, phenomenological, and ethnographic studies of teaching.[22]
Inquiry methods used in such studies have a potential for improving the
quality of appraisal efforts.

Of the four purposes of evaluation of teaching, none is more important
than long-range support of an instructor's continuing education. Self-study
and career development need to be undertaken with a commitment to institutional goals, awareness of existing instructional conditions, and a certain
expectation of the results of alternative pedagogies. The campus should provide a supportive environment for professional growth, partly by making
periodic review of purposes, attending to the findings of research on instructional processes, and ensuring fair (though subjective) judgments of teaching

quality. It is an administrative obligation usually best discharged by evaluation so cleverly devised that the individual instructor is left better informed and even more in charge of instruction than before.

Notes

1. Administrators and faculties under pressure cannot be counted on to protect academic freedom. For college-level teaching, an embarrassing portrayal is Schrecker (1986).
2. Take the criterial item "always explains things thoroughly." It sounds good, but inventor Edwin Land reminds us that some teachers explain too much, needing occasionally to just show wonder (Beckman Lecture, November 21, 1985, University of Illinois).
3. For many years student ratings of instruction were berated by professors as subjective and unknowing. A 1969 University of Illinois CRUEL Committee chaired by Richard Anderson carefully examined the research literature and found that although student ratings were subjective and based on limited knowledge, they had substantial validity. Probably just as valid today, student ratings of instruction are now widely tolerated, and even sometimes taken quite seriously.
4. The most sophisticated measures of college learning are measures of aptitude to learn, not measures of attained achievement. They indicate rather accurately which students have learned the most in past years and who will learn the most in the future, but they do not tell how effectively the course has been taught (Stake, 1995).
5. Seldom is there any listing of impropriety unless it has been decided that a formal case is to be made against the professor.
6. According to Seldin (1993) nearly all colleges and universities in the United States collect and use student ratings of instruction.
7. In the Duties-Based-Teacher Evaluation Approach, a minimum level of achievement is required on every one of the listed dimensions. Teacher performance is measured using more than one source of evidence, and the teacher "has the opportunity to respond to all evidence . . . and to appeal against any decision" (p. 34). Consistent and significant inaccuracies are used as a correction factor and as evidence of bias. Evidence involves judgments, records, observations, test data, teacher portfolios, and footprint data.
8. As Doyle (1982) mentions, "It seems most unlikely that any one set of characteristics will apply with equal force to teaching of all kinds of material to all kinds of students under all kinds of circumstance. . . . To try to prepare such a list entails substantial risk" (p. 27).
9. This constitutes a serious problem since "the central issue in validity is the appraisal of meaning and consequences" (Messick, 1989, p. 14).
10. Challenging an instructor who criticized contemporary evaluations of college teaching, Michael Theall and Jennifer Franklin (1990) used Robert Ebel's words (1983, p. 65): "No corner of the university lacks faculty members who fulminate against student evaluations, with little or no examination of the large body of research . . . that underlies the practice." Such challenges are common by evaluation researchers who are also administrators of faculty evaluation systems. But the body of research Ebel referred to mostly looks narrowly at the reliability of representing student views, not so much at full representation of merit in teaching. This too is a bias.
11. We were drawn to the moral of Tolstoy's story of Anna Karenina (1877), a story of star-crossed love but concluding with the claim that the distinguishing characteristic of human consciousness is its ability to know good and bad, not as discovered or calculated knowledge, not as infallible and not always accessible, but ingrained and evolving in each person's experience.

12. A substantial body of research has been conducted along this line of inquiry. Most of it has focused on methods and sources of information regarding teaching effectiveness, especially on the use of students as raters (Kinney and Smith, 1992; Braskamp, Brandenburg, and Ory, 1984; Cashin, 1988; Marsh, 1987; El-Hassan, 1995).

13. A community of practice can be defined as "a group of professionals, informally bound to one another through exposure to a common class of problems, common pursuit of solutions, and thereby themselves embodying a store of knowledge" (Johnson-Letz and Johnson-Letz, 1998). Communities of practice have been traced back to the European guilds, but some writers see them as old as human interactivity of any kind (Community Intelligence Labs, 1998).

14. At Xerox, John Seely Brown found unexpected ways for autonomous, greatly reluctant photocopy repairmen to talk with each other about fixing ever changing models of copiers. We college teachers are probably as smart as they. We should find collective ways of addressing our teaching problems and connecting the evaluation of classroom teaching with the maintenance and repair of departmental instruction.

15. "Learning is not only an activity, but also a vehicle for engagement with others. Learning is a social phenomenon. We all belong to communities of practice (work, school, in personal activities). It is through membership in communities of practice that we come to know—and become empowered by what we know. The social world is where work gets done, where learning takes place. Instructors encompass an ensemble of interconnected communities of practice whose boundaries do not necessarily (or usually) follow the formal boundaries of the organization" (Alpert, 1998).

16. "In a strong department, a high priority is given to collective decisions about what needs to be done. Each member has her own priorities but reallocation of priorities is needed when reconsidering the mission of the department as a whole. Some members of a department make unique contributions to collegiality and shared purpose, attending to the local scene rather than to gaining national prominence as individuals. Wise institutions recognize and support emerging communities of practice" (Alpert, 1998).

17. Loomis recognized individual professional performance but also placed great value on qualities that held the community together. The Loomis list ranked individuals in terms of individual contribution to the department. At one time at the top of the list was a Nobel Prize winner, so placed not for intellect but for his powerful contributions to other members of the department. (Alpert, 1998).

18. George's case is part of an internal study: "Trade-Offs: The Use of Student Ratings Results and Its Possible Impact on Instructional Improvement." In order to ensure confidentiality, pseudonyms were used.

19. "In general, the course, which is taught by a number of different faculty members, does not receive good ratings. Since the course is required and is mathematically oriented, ratings are not typically as high as they might be in other courses. In other courses, students might have some latitude in their response to a particular situation. More than one response might be acceptable. In an analytically oriented course, there is much less latitude. An answer is usually either right or wrong. There are fewer shades of gray" (Dr. Edwards, one of George's peers).

20. To identify evaluation responsibilities here, it is desirable to call some people administrators and others teachers. Obviously all teachers have administrative responsibility, and some administrators are members of the instructional staff. It is not implied that administrative and instructional responsibilities should be assigned to separate people. For convenience here, we oversimplify the two roles: administration and teaching. Thus, teachers on committees are administrators as well as instructors.

21. Many writers treat autonomy as a barrier to school improvement, but its merit is well argued and illustrated by Schön (1982).

22. See, for example, Denny (1978) and Smith and Geoffrey (1978).

References

Alpert, D. A. "Representation of Quality." Seminar lecture in Theories of Educational Evaluation, University of Illinois, Feb. 23, 1998.

Amidon, E., and Hunter, E. *Improving Teaching.* New York: Holt, Rinehart and Winston, 1966.

Association for Curriculum and Supervision and Curriculum Development. *Using What We Know about Teaching.* Washington, D.C.: Association for Curriculum and Supervision and Curriculum Development, 1984.

Berlak, H., and others. T. *Toward a New Science of Educational Testing and Assessment.* Albany, N.Y.: State University of New York Press, 1992.

Borich, G. D. *The Appraisal of Teaching.* Reading, Mass.: Addison-Wesley, 1977.

Braskamp, L. A., Brandenburg, D. C., and Ory, J. C. *Evaluating Teaching Effectiveness.* Thousand Oaks, Calif.: Sage, 1984.

Braskamp L., and Ory, J. *Assessing Faculty Work.* San Francisco: Jossey-Bass, 1994.

Broudy, H. S. "Historic Exemplars of Teaching Method." In N. L. Gage (ed.), *Handbook of Research on Teaching.* Chicago: Rand McNally, 1963.

Brown, J. S. "Common Sense of Purpose." In *What Is a Community of Practice?* Community Intelligence Labs. [http://www.co-i-l.com/coil/knowledge-garden/cop/definitions.shtml]. 1997.

Cashin, W. E. *Student Ratings of Teaching: A Summary of the Research.* Manhattan: Kansas State University, Center for Faculty Evaluation and Development, 1988.

Cave, M., Hanney, S., Kogan, M., and Travett, G. *The Use of Performance Indicators in Higher Education: A Critical Analysis of Developing Practice.* London: Kingsley, 1988.

Cisneros-Cohernour, E. J. "Trade-offs: The Use of Student Ratings Results and Its Possible Impact on Instructional Improvement." Unpublished report, University of Illinois, 1997.

Community Intelligence Labs. Communities of Practice. [http://www.co-i-l.com/coil /knowledge-garden/cop/index.shtml]. 1997.

Cronbach, L. J., and Gleser, G. *Psychological Tests and Personnel Decisions.* Urbana: University of Illinois Press, 1965.

Denny, T. "Some Still Do." In R. E. Stake and J. A. Easley (eds.), *Case Studies in Science Education.* 1978.

Doyle, K. O., Jr. *Evaluating Teaching.* San Francisco: New Lexington Press, 1982.

Dunkin, M. J., and Biddle, B. J. *The Study of Teaching.* Austin, Tex.: Holt, Rinehart & Winston, 1974.

Eble, K. E. *The Aims of College Teaching.* San Francisco: Jossey-Bass, 1983.

El Hassan, K. "Students' Ratings of Instruction: Generalizability of Findings." *Studies in Education,* 1995, *21,* 411–429.

Feldman K. A. "Instructional Effectiveness of College Teachers as Judged by Teachers Themselves, Current Students, Colleagues, Administrators, and External (Neutral Observers)." *Research in Higher Education,* 1989, *30,* 137–172.

Fetterman, D. M., and Pitman, M. A. *Educational Evaluation: Ethnography in Theory, Practice, and Politics.* Thousand Oaks, Calif.: Sage, 1986.

Gardner, H. *Frames of Mind: The Theory of Multiple Intelligences.* New York: Basic Books, 1983.

Genova, W. J., Madoff, M. J., Chink, R., and Thomas, G. B. *Mutual Benefit Evaluation of Faculty and Administrators in Higher Education.* New York: Ballinger, 1976.

Jaeger, R. "World Class Standards, Choice, and Privatization: Weak Measurement Serving Presumptive Policy." Vice presidential address to the American Educational Research Association, San Francisco, 1992.

Johnson-Letz, P., and Johnson-Letz, T. "Bonding by Exposure to Common Problems." In *What Is a Community of Practice?* Community Intelligence Labs. [http://www.co-i-l.com/coil/knowledge-garden/cop/definitions.shtml]. 1997.

Kinney, D. P., and Smith, S. P. "Age and Teaching Performance." *Journal of Higher Education*, 1992, *63*, 282–302.

Land, E. "The Experimental Bases of the Retinex Theory of Color Vision." Beckman Lecture, University of Illinois, November 21, 1985.

Mabry, L. *Portfolios Plus: A Critical Guide to Alternative Assessments and Portfolios.* Thousand Oaks, Calif.: Corwin Press, 1999.

Marsh, H. W. "Students' Evaluations of University Teaching: Research Findings, Methodological Issues, and Directions for Future Research." *International Journal of Educational Research*, 1987, *11*, 253–388.

Marton F., and Säljö, R. "Outcome and Process." *British Journal of Educational Psychology*, 1976, *46*, 4–11.

Messick, S. L. "Validity." In R. L. Linn (ed.), *Educational Measurement*. (3rd ed.) New York: American Council on Education and Macmillan, 1989.

Meyer, J. W., Scott, R. W., and Deal, T. E. "Institutional and Technical Sources of Organizational Structure: Explaining the Structure of Educational Organizations." In H. D. Stein (ed.), *Organization and the Human Services*. Philadelphia: Temple University Press, 1981.

Millman, J. "Criterion Referenced Measurement." In W. James Popham (ed.), *Evaluation in Education*. Berkeley, Calif.: McCutchan, 1974.

Office of Instructional Resources. *Faculty Handbook of Teaching Evaluation*. Urbana: University of Illinois, 1989.

Peters, T. J., and Waterman, R. H., Jr. *In Search of Excellence*. New York: Warner, 1984.

Porter, A. "External Standards and Good Teaching." *Educational Evaluation and Policy Analysis*, 1989, *11*, 354.

Romberg, T. A. (ed.). *Reform in School Mathematics and Authentic Assessment*. Albany, N.Y.: State University of New York Press, 1995.

Ryans, D. G. *Characteristics of Teachers*. Washington, D.C.: American Council on Education, 1960.

Schön, D. *The Reflective Practitioner*. New York: Basic Books, 1982.

Schrecker, E. *No Ivory Tower: McCarthyism and the Universities*. New York: Oxford University Press, 1986.

Scriven, M. "The Evaluation of Teachers and Teaching." *California Journal of Education Research*, 1974, *15*, 109–115.

Scriven, M. "The State of the Art in Tertiary Teacher Evaluation." *Research and Development in Higher Education*, 1988, *10*, 2–27.

Scriven M. *Evaluating Teachers as Professionals*. Perth: University of Western Australia, 1994.

Scriven, M. "A Unified Theory Approach to Teacher Evaluation." *Studies in Educational Evaluation*, 1995, *21*, 111–129.

Seldin, P. "How Colleges Evaluate Professors: 1983 versus 1993." *AAHE Bulletin*, 1993, *12*, 6–8.

Shulman, L. "Knowledge and Teaching: Foundations of the New Reform." *Harvard Education Review*, 1986, *57*, 1–22.

Smith, L. M., and Geoffrey, K. L. *The Complexities of an Urban Classroom: An Analysis Toward General Theory of Teaching*. New York: Rinehart and Winston, 1968.

Stake, R. "The Invalidity of Standardized Testing for Measuring Mathematics Achievement." In T. A. Romberg (ed.), *Reform in School Mathematics and Authentic Assessment*. Albany: State University of New York Press, 1995.

Stake, R., and others. "The Evolving Syntheses of Program Value." *Evaluation Practice*, *18*(2), 1997, 2, 89–103.

Tolstoy, L. *Anna Karenina*. New York: Penguin, 1877.

Wenger, E. "Communities of Practice: Where Learning Happens." *Benchmarks*, Fall 1991, pp. 6–8.

ROBERT E. STAKE *is emeritus professor and director of the Center for Instructional Research and Curriculum Evaluation at the College of Education, University of Illinois at Urbana-Champaign.*

EDITH J. CISNEROS-COHERNOUR *is a doctoral candidate in evaluation and higher education at the University of Illinois at Urbana-Champaign and an associate professor at the Autonomous University of Yucatan.*

6

The University of Nebraska at Lincoln's peer review project is described and critiqued as a guide to others planning on using the process.

An Examination of the Implementation of Peer Review of Teaching

Daniel J. Bernstein, Jessica Jonson, Karen Smith

Peer review of teaching will likely play an increasing role in the summative arena as well as its current formative use. This chapter offers a description of a campuswide program to provide faculty with an opportunity to undertake substantive peer review of a course. The model of interaction was derived directly from the American Association for Higher Education (AAHE) project on peer review (Hutchings, 1996b), which has an explicitly formative flavor. We will describe what the faculty participants did and also report some of our observations of the impact of participation on those faculty and their students. Based on these observations, we will offer some suggestions for improving the implementation of peer review of teaching and also describe some likely future directions for peer interactions on teaching.

AAHE Peer Review Model

In 1994 the AAHE Teaching Initiative began a project on peer review of teaching that included representatives from twelve universities. As documented by the project leadership team (Hutchings, 1995, 1996a), faculty from the twelve campuses worked on individual versions of a general model

Note: This project was supported by grants from the Fund for the Improvement of Post Secondary Education (U.S. Department of Education), the University of Nebraska Teaching Council, and the University of Nebraska Pepsi Quasi-endowment Fund. We are especially grateful to Joan Leitzel and Rick Edwards for their support and encouragement and to Bob Brown for consistently excellent counsel. The chapter is dedicated to the memory of Al Kilgore, whose vision remains our beacon.

of peer interaction and consultation about the teaching of a particular course. Faculty working in pairs within academic disciplines exchanged written materials in three categories. The first interaction focused on the intellectual content of a course, including the statement of course goals, a rationale for the inclusion of those goals, and an account of the intellectual decisions that went into the construction of the course. The faculty members exchanged annotated syllabi and narrative accounts of the creation of the courses, offering written comments to each other on what they read.

The second interaction focused on teaching practice in the identified course. Each faculty member identified in writing specific goals for class or other contact time with students, along with a rationale for the planned activities. The peer colleague made several visits to those settings, followed by written comments about how well the planned goals were accomplished. This approach is explicitly not normative; the feedback from a peer is about the accomplishment of one's own goals, not a comparison with a hypothetical ideal class or teacher. As with the first interaction, the written comments are exchanged privately between the peers for their own use.

The third interaction focused on student learning, that is, what kind of understanding students reached about the course material and how many students achieved identified levels of understanding. Faculty members exchanged copies of examinations, written assignments, and project descriptions that were used to assess the level of student achievement in the class, along with examples of actual student performance. Whenever possible, the faculty members also provided examples of the feedback given to students on their performance—both grades and suggestions or explanations. Peers read the materials and offered comments on the quality of the understanding asked for, the depth of understanding students actually achieved, and the usefulness of the feedback given to learners.

The emphasis on the effects of teaching was the most unusual of the three components of the AAHE peer review model. Faculty are accustomed to discussions of course content in individual conversations with disciplinary peers and in the occasional documents provided to curriculum committees that oversee the nominal content of courses. In general, however, faculty hold themselves responsible for presenting coherent, appropriate, and accessible material in their discipline and students responsible for the amount they learn (as a function of their ability, motivation, prior preparation, and time available). The AAHE model pushed the limits of faculty culture by suggesting that faculty are in some way accountable for the effects of their teaching on the understanding of learners.

University of Nebraska–Lincoln Peer Review Project

The seven faculty from the University of Nebraska–Lincoln (UNL) who participated in the original AAHE project were uniformly positive about the experience. The quality of time talking with colleagues about teaching was very high, and all individuals found benefits to their own teaching from both receiving a colleague's reactions and the process of learning about the peer's teaching. Over a three-year period, thirty additional faculty members engaged in the basic three-step process. Each year's faculty recipients participated in a two-week-long seminar with all the pairs at the end of the academic year to review the project activities and to discuss teaching at UNL in general.

Monitoring the Process and Outcomes

Because administrative support for the project came from the Fund for the Improvement of Post Secondary Education (FIPSE), which always expects a strong evaluation component, many layers of data were collected during the course of the project. To inform the development of measures and to guide the evaluation of the project, a general model of the possible impact of peer review was articulated by the project team. Figure 6.1 shows a schematic diagram of the possible interactions and influences that the team anticipated might occur. For each conceptual component of the process identified, an operational measure was developed that was intended to track that feature as shown in the figure.

At the left side of Figure 6.1 is the peer review process itself, consisting of three written interactions and a two-week summer seminar in teaching. Possible effects of this intervention were tracked in three areas: classroom practice, teacher and student attitudes and motivation, and course materials. These factors should all contribute to student learning, which is the final measure at the right side of Figure 6.1.

The experience of peer review was assumed to influence student learning through an indirect route. There could be direct influence on instructor attitudes, instructional practices, and classroom practices, which could influence student attitudes and motivation directly. Student attitudes and motivation are assumed to be the main direct influence on learning, while instructional and classroom practices may also have a direct effect on learning. The figure lists the measures used for each assumed component of the process.

For each participating fellow, these measures were taken at least once before and at least once after participation in the peer review interactions. Given that faculty teaching assignments change frequently and unexpectedly (even when stability was assured), it was not possible to keep the number of observations exactly equal for all faculty. Our examination of the project is actually based on pre- and postintervention data from twenty-three faculty members who taught significant numbers of undergraduate students and for whom we had sufficient data. The range of data gathered allow examination of how participation in the program influenced several features of teaching performance and student participation, as well as how effective the teaching was in changing student understanding.

Figure 6.1. Peer Review Model

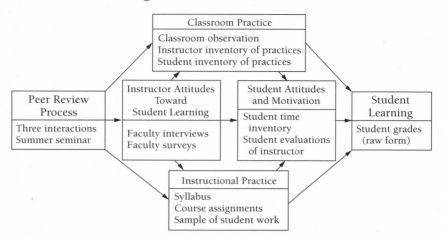

Impact on Student Achievement. When all participants are viewed as a group, there was not a systematic, consistent change in student achievement attributable to peer review. There were faculty whose students demonstrated higher achievement in their courses after participation than before, but the students of over half of the faculty sample showed no increase in learning after peer review. It is worth noting that these were not neophyte teachers who could readily improve their effectiveness every time a class is offered. Despite their level of experience, only one of the twenty-three faculty for whom we had adequate data showed a noticeable decline in student achievement after participation. Perhaps that is less regression in student performance than one might expect merely by chance.

We examined the teaching practices of those faculty whose students showed better understanding after peer review to see if there were any consistent changes in their practices that might be related to the improved work by learners. Two changed features of teaching were associated with improved learning in our sample of faculty: quality of feedback to learners and raising expectations of student performance. In one cluster of six peer review participants, we identified a consistent improvement in student achievement. As shown in Figure 6.2 there were more high-achieving students in these instructors' classes after peer review than before. Figure 6.3 shows data from students' reports of the usefulness of feedback received from the same faculty, also before and after their participation in peer review. The frequency of ratings in the two lowest categories decreased substantially, while the frequency of ratings of the two high-utility categories both increased.

Another cluster of eight faculty was identified that also had consistent improvement in student achievement. Figure 6.4 shows the achievement data for these faculty. The biggest difference is the increase in students who

Figure 6.2. Student Achievement in Course Work, Before and After Faculty Participation in Peer Review Program

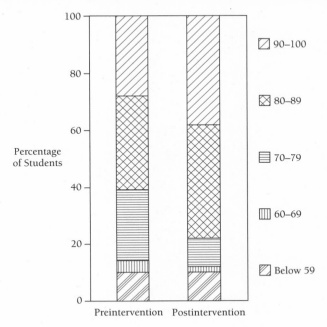

Note: Represents six faculty.

achieved in the 80–89 percent correct range. All three of the lowest categories decreased, and the top category remained about the same. Examination of this cluster of faculty revealed that they had in common a noticeable shift in the level of cognitive understanding they were requiring in their course. Figure 6.5 shows that the amount of rote or comprehension assessment used declined after participation in peer review, with substantial increases in the amount of application, analysis, synthesis, and evaluation required by assignments. These faculty reported in project meetings that peer review had led them to reexamine their course assessments, and if anything, they expected an overall decrease in achievement of these more difficult goals. In fact, their students achieved a higher percentage correct than did students who had taken the courses with the less challenging assessment.

Although these results were not universal, perhaps the observed patterns of selectively changed achievement suggest some features of peer review that could be emphasized in future seminars.

Impact on Student Attitudes and Motivation. In the model of peer review we described, the immediate source of student learning comes from the efforts and perceptions of the learners. Faculty teaching practices would have their influence on learning in part by arranging a context in which

Figure 6.3. Ratings of Usefulness of Feedback for Faculty, Before and After Participation in Peer Review Program

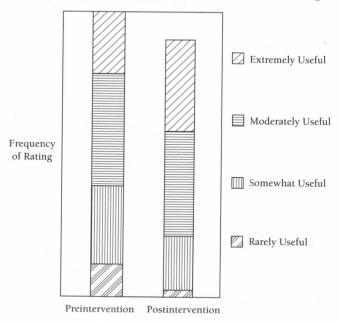

Note: Represents six faculty.

students engage in productive learning activities with greater intensity or focus than previously. Accordingly, we examined student perceptions and activity to see if the collective efforts of the faculty had resulted in changes in what students felt or did.

There was no evidence that changes in faculty performance had consistent effects on student attitudes or motivation. None of the comparisons of student survey responses showed a systematic pattern of change from before peer review began to afterward.

The most important finding from the student surveys came from the items that asked students to report how much time they spent in preparation for various aspects of the course. On a variety of specific questions, students consistently reported spending considerably less time on out-of-class preparation than even the most modest faculty expectation, and only a rare student reported spending the mythical two hours outside class for every hour in class. Like the attitude measures, these reports showed no change across the semester.

Because the project staff gave all faculty participants complete accounts of the data collected in their classes, each year's group of faculty became aware of the apparently low level of student effort, and there emerged among faculty a stream of consistently critical commentary about students.

Figure 6.4. Student Achievement in Course Work, Before and After Faculty Participation in Peer Review Project

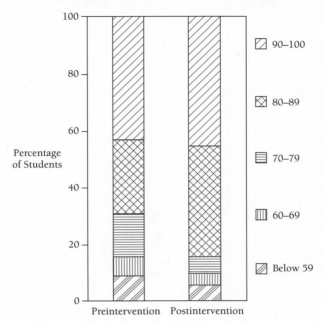

Note: Represents eight faculty.

This backlash from the reported time measure was one of the most striking effects of the process, and the data further mitigated against faculty's assuming greater responsibility for student success. We have tried to make the discussion of these data an occasion for faculty to examine teaching practices that are more and less supportive of consistently high student effort, but that was not always successful. As a result of these data and the subsequent discussions, student time on task has become one of the focal points of our collective peer conversations about teaching practices and learning.

Impact on Faculty Attitudes and Practices. The model of peer review suggests that the student attitudes and actions result in part from the instructor's attitudes toward teaching and learning and in part from the collection of teaching practices arranged by the instructor. Given that we found no systematic change in student attitudes or behavior from peer review of faculty, we asked whether the peer review process had an impact on the faculty themselves.

Attitudes. Overall, the attitude of faculty toward the peer review project itself was extraordinarily positive. All of the original participants completed the entire sequence of activities, and they reported enjoying the seminar far more than they had expected. The opportunity to discuss substantive issues around teaching with colleagues proved to be highly stimulating. Rather

Figure 6.5. Frequency of Assessment in Conceptual Level for Faculty, Before and After Participation in Peer Review Project.

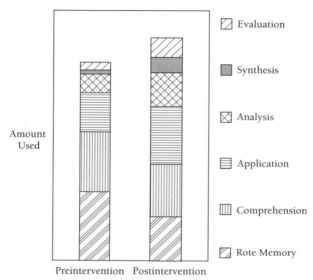

Note: Represents eight faculty.

than being seen as a burden, this process was widely regarded as an opportunity to spend time on development of teaching.

Despite all the goodwill generated by and toward the peer review process, there was little or no change in faculty attitudes toward student learning or faculty responsibility for student learning. In general, the seminar discussions did not alter the basic faculty view that students are responsible for learning and that attitude remains a cornerstone of a typical teaching philosophy. There was also no change in the traditional faculty attitudes about grading; the dominant view remained that grades should primarily reflect relative standing among students so they can be differentiated based on their performance. The notion of criterion-referenced grading that puts student achievement ahead of student ranking was not widely adopted, despite extended discussion of the issue in the seminar.

In-Class Teaching Practices. Several individual faculty members dramatically changed their class practices as a result of their participation in peer review. In all of those cases, the amount of time they spent lecturing (measured by observation and by self-report) decreased substantially, and active participation (often group work) increased dramatically. For most faculty, however, there was no systematic change away from the conventional class in which the instructor does most of the talking. The amount of time needed to generate new class plans is significantly greater than the amount of time needed to refine a set of lecture notes, and it proved exceedingly difficult to motivate faculty to undertake sweeping revision of their time with learners. Faculty who did change their use of class time had mixed results on student learning, with some showing increases in student achievement and others not.

Assignments and Evaluation of Students. Our examination of the collected course materials from the faculty revealed some interesting changes in teaching practice, though not consistently. About half of the faculty required students to do lab projects or term papers in stages, but the prevalence of that practice was unaffected by participation in peer review. In the peer review seminar, the effectiveness of a range of teaching strategies was presented and discussed by each group at length, but faculty reported that in the end, their choices were driven more by limitations on their time than by potential increases in student achievement.

There was a clear increase in the number of faculty who asked students to demonstrate higher-order intellectual skills and critical thinking. Our examination of the level of understanding required by assignments showed that following peer review, about half of the faculty participants added assignments that asked for application, analysis, and evaluation of material, and many faculty decreased the percentage of their assessments based on rote learning or simple comprehension. Faculty clearly do value intellectual depth, and many used their interaction with peers to reexamine their own assessment practices.

There was also a cluster of faculty who increased the quality of the feedback they gave to students on assignments. We examined both the quantity and the quality of the feedback provided on examinations, projects, and papers, and there was a cluster of faculty who increased either the quality or the quantity of what they wrote to students when course work was returned. Although not all faculty showed an increase, none showed a decrease in the amount or quality of feedback. Overall the impact of peer review of quality feedback to students was modest but positive.

Those faculty who chose to increase the cognitive complexity of their assessments and those who improved the quality of the feedback they gave on assignments tended to be the faculty whose students increased their level of achievement. There is no support in these observations to suggest that these features of teaching were the cause of the increased achievement, but they seemed to be the two most useful markers of changed teachers in our sample of peer review participants.

Summary of Impact on Faculty. Overall there were no large, pervasive, or consistent changes in faculty attitudes toward learning or in teaching methods that followed the process of peer review. This process of formative interaction followed by a brief summer seminar did not overwhelm all the other factors that influence faculty choices about teaching. However, about a third of the participants made significant changes in some individual component of their teaching, and they typically attributed their decision to initiate change to the process of peer review. Those were also typically the faculty whose learners showed improved achievement. It is interesting to note that the virtually universal enthusiasm for the peer review process translated into changed teaching practices for only a minority of participants, and perhaps as a result there was only selective impact on the learners in this project. Programs that report warm reception from faculty as their primary outcome may wish in the future to target changes in practice as an additional critical index of success.

Increasing the Impact of Peer Review

Given the original goals of the project, it was somewhat disappointing to find uneven results on student learning and achievement. All faculty participants embraced the program and engaged each other in meaningful interactions and consultations on teaching. Some faculty took the conversation to the next level and made substantive changes in their courses that resulted in improved levels of student understanding, although most others recognized the potential benefits of developing new teaching practices but chose not to make substantive changes in their teaching.

An understanding of this choice begins with explicit recognition of learner responsibility for education. Faculty believe that students' actions and choices are the major determinant of their success in higher education. Our background reviews of teaching literature confirmed that student time on task, ability, and previous preparation consistently account for more variance in outcomes than do most features of teaching. Faculty typically will feel comfortable in a conversation about learning only if the campus culture makes it clear that students' first priority should be spending time on their studies. Without acknowledgment of that premise, it will be very hard to engage many faculty in extensive efforts to improve student understanding by changing or developing their teaching practices.

Within the smaller portion of the variance in learning that is attributable to teaching practices, however, there is plenty of room for faculty growth, and our challenge is to identify what form of peer review program might increase the percentage of faculty who change their teaching practices in ways that would influence student learning. Programs like supplemental instruction (Martin and Arendale, 1994) show sizable increases in student achievement despite relatively poor preparation, and mastery or competence-based teaching approaches (Kulik, Kulik, and Bangert-Drowns, 1990) greatly improve achievement by increasing learner motivation and time on task. Given that our participants read about and discussed these programs, it was discouraging that virtually no faculty in our sample added these teaching practices to their courses. The changes made were much more modest refinements of existing practices rather than fundamental change in course structure or attitude toward learning.

Our conversations with participants over the four years of the project revealed that faculty have no reason to believe that they will be either rewarded for good student achievement or held accountable for poor achievement. The most common contingency on teaching seems to be that consistently high ratings by students will result in the best feedback from the institution on the teaching portion of professional work. When global ratings of satisfaction with the course and instructor are higher than local averages, faculty are considered good teachers for purposes of annual review. Even in the materials requested for teaching awards, the majority of attention is given to testimonial evidence, either by students or from faculty who often relay student comments. Comment on the intellectual quality of the work done is not routinely required in such portfolios, and evidence of sustained high achievement by learners is rarely asked for or provided. If anything, in most faculty circles consistently high student performance is taken as evidence of low standards, usually without review of the assessments used or the work generated by learners.

It may simply be the case that peer review of teaching (or any other program intended to improve student understanding and achievement) will succeed only when community standards expect and require evidence of impact on student learning. Department and college leaders need to honor evidence of exceptional achievement in learning in all the ways that faculty recognize (annual review, tenure, promotion, and awards). Once learning outcomes are important to faculty, there is a greater likelihood that they will choose to implement the practices they learned about through peer review.

Implications for Improvement

Inevitably there is some conflict between the formative and summative roles of peer review of teaching (Cavanagh, 1996), since the first step in growing as a teacher is the frank identification of areas that could use development. Including such self-assessment in personnel materials for evaluation is unlikely to be rewarded, so having a summative function of peer review could be seen as diminishing the formative value of the process. We believe it is possible to save the baby and the bathwater in this case by using alternating periods of development and evaluation. If faculty have access to resources and time for formative peer review that is shielded from scrutiny for periods of a few years, they can generate substantial improvement in teaching that can be brought forward during periodic times of accountability. This kind of structure has been used successfully within an academic unit (Bernstein, 1996) to build a firewall between the two classes of peer interactions, allowing faculty enough unscrutinized space to explore their teaching honestly while also providing clear occasions for evaluation of the effectiveness of current practice.

It appears that a key feature of the ongoing peer review process at UNL is the voluntary nature of participation. As a formative exercise and an opportunity to generate evidence for summative purposes, faculty participate only when they have an individual goal to accomplish. In both cases, the process keeps the focus on student understanding. In the formative case, faculty work to upgrade the level of understanding, in what they ask for and what students can demonstrate; in the summative case, faculty would be given credit for the adoption of teaching practices that have a demonstrated impact on the quality and quantity of student learning.

Future Directions for Peer Review

The uses of peer consultation and interaction about teaching and learning are in principle endless; they could be seen as parallel to the many ways that faculty interact with each other about other forms of intellectual work, such as research in laboratory and field settings. It has been said that to have great poets, one must have great audiences, and the same may be true in teaching. Only when the feedback we get on teaching comes from intellectual peers (not simply from interested novices) will the level of our work grow to its greatest potential.

At UNL we are continuing our work with peer review in two new directions. First, peer review fellowships are being given to departmental teams of faculty who teach courses in the core undergraduate curriculum of a discipline or program. These faculty engage in the usual forms of interaction focused on their individual courses, including the extensive look at student learning. Among the questions asked in that part of the conversation is whether the learning observed is appropriate for the curriculum and the general goals of the major program. This kind of conversation is especially useful in disciplines that have meaningful prerequisite orderings among their courses. All parties have a clear interest in holding specific conversations around the understanding and achievement of students in courses that are gateways to any organized curriculum. As an extension of this idea, we plan to form interdisciplinary faculty teams to examine the same student materials for evidence of performance congruent with the goals of our general education program.

Second, we are developing a community of faculty who are willing to read integrated documents that give evidence about teaching and learning; those readers could in principle provide an independent, arm's-length evaluation of the substance of the evidence provided. This development proceeds slowly but steadily. As a first step, peer review fellows are asked to integrate their three separate written peer review interactions into a coherent and concise document that summarizes the results of their sustained inquiry into their course. These documents are an evolving form of what is being called a course portfolio (Cerbin, 1994, 1996; Hutchings, 1998), and they give an account of teaching practices used to accomplish specific learning goals and what kind of understanding was achieved. The second step involves faculty's voluntarily sharing those documents with local colleagues to get feedback on them as records of their work. Once they are comfortable with their work, we circulate the documents to colleagues in the same discipline at other universities for their comments on the intellectual quality of the material presented and the understanding asked for and demonstratèd by students. These independent evaluations will be crucial to the use of course portfolios as evidence of exceptional scholarly work in teaching.

These evolving processes of faculty peer review at UNL will continue to be supported. In the short term, the benefits have been clear, but mostly for the faculty participants. An improved sense of community and the chance to develop teaching in a professional way are desirable outcomes already achieved. It is also likely that the process will be influential in the way teaching is regarded in personnel decisions. Having credible peer-reviewed representations of the intellectual work in teaching could potentially increase its impact in the process. It will be especially important to include evidence of student learning as a central part of the representation of effective teaching. The individual cases of faculty in our project who improved their conceptual goals and student understanding are sufficiently encouraging to merit continued refinement and implementation of peer review. We hope to extend the effectiveness of the process to a larger percentage of our participating peer review fellows. The search for broad impact on student learning will also continue as a longer-term goal. We believe students will derive more benefit from the process when peer-reviewed evidence of student understanding is a major criterion for summative evaluation of teaching.

References

Bernstein, D. J. "A Departmental System for Balancing the Development and Evaluation of College Teaching." *Innovative Higher Education*, 1996, *20*, 241–248.

Cavanagh, R. R. "Formative and Summative Evaluation in the Faculty Peer Review of Teaching." *Innovative Higher Education*, 1996, *20*, 235–240.

Cerbin, W. "The Course Portfolio as a Tool for Continuous Improvement of Teaching and Learning." *Journal on Excellence in College Teaching*, 1994, *5*, 95–105.

Cerbin, W. "Inventing a New Genre: The Course Portfolio at the University of Wisconsin-La Crosse." In P. Hutchings (ed.), *Making Teaching Community Property*. Washington, D.C.: American Association for Higher Education, 1996.

Hutchings, P. (ed.). *From Idea to Prototype: The Peer Review of Teaching*. Washington, D.C.: American Association for Higher Education, 1995.

Hutchings, P. "The Peer Review of Teaching: Progress, Issues, and Prospects." *Innovative Higher Education*, 1996a, *20*, 221–234.

Hutchings, P. (ed.). *Making Teaching Community Property*. Washington, D.C.: American Association for Higher Education, 1996b.

Hutchings, P. (ed.). *The Course Portfolio*. Washington, D.C.: American Association for Higher Education, 1998.

Kulik, C. C., Kulik, J. A., and Bangert-Drowns, R. L. "Effectiveness of Mastery Learning Programs: A Meta-Analysis." *Review of Educational Research*, 1990, *60*, 265–299.

Martin, D. C., and Arendale, D. R. (eds.). Supplemental Instruction: Increasing Achievement and Retention. New Directions in Teaching and Learning, no. 60. San Francisco: Jossey-Bass, 1994.

DANIEL J. BERNSTEIN is professor of psychology at the University of Nebraska—Lincoln and a Carnegie Scholar in the Carnegie Academy for the Scholarship of Teaching and Learning.

JESSICA JONSON is the coordinator of University-wide Assessment of Student Outcomes at the University of Nebraska—Lincoln.

KAREN SMITH is assistant professor of psychology at Truman State University.

7

Colleagues, perhaps through special faculty committees,
can play an important part in evaluating teaching
portfolios, especially for summative decisions.

Evaluating the Teaching Portfolio: A Role for Colleagues

John A. Centra

Although the rewards for research are often cited as the reason that teaching is undervalued in many colleges and universities, other reasons may well be more critical. The lack of information and evidence about teaching performance is one. Another is having valid means to judge that evidence if and when it is collected.

The teaching portfolio has been promoted as a vehicle for collecting and documenting information about an individual's teaching performance. But the problem of how best to assess the information has not yet been addressed adequately. This chapter describes how one group, a teacher's colleagues, can provide valid assessments of portfolios and similar self-reported information on teaching.

The Portfolio and Teacher Self-Reports

The teaching portfolio has been adapted from such fields as art and architecture, in which professionals display samples of their work for clients or employers. In the mid-1980s a similar product was called a teaching dossier and was defined as a "summary of a professor's major teaching accomplishments and strengths" (Shore and others, 1986). A project to identify the kinds of information a faculty member might include in a teaching dossier was sponsored by the Canadian Association of University Teachers. The project report suggested three major areas containing forty-nine specific items (Shore and others, 1986):

NEW DIRECTIONS FOR TEACHING AND LEARNING, no. 83, Fall 2000   © Jossey-Bass, a Wiley company

Products of good teaching such as student workbooks, completed assignments, and pre- and postexamination results.
Materials developed by the teacher, such as syllabli, curriculum and teaching aids, and innovations, and an evaluation of their success
Assessments from others, such as students, colleagues, or alumni

Entries included by a teacher in a portfolio can represent both good or
bad practices, or they may be more selective and display only the best work
(Wolf, 1991). Most teaching portfolios seem to include only positive examples, especially when they are being used in personnel decisions. When a
portfolio is being used for summative purposes, it is reasonable to expect
teachers to provide only positive examples and thereby make their best case
for reviewers. Expecting teachers to reveal their faults in this instance is not
only unrealistic but unfair to those willing to expose their weaknesses.

An important element of the portfolio emphasized in an American
Association for Higher Education (AAHE) monograph is the teachers' reflections on their actions (Edgerton, Hutchings, and Quinlan, 1991). The ideal
portfolio, they argue, would include the professor's reflections about instructional decisions, thereby capturing the rationale and thinking behind these
decisions. In his classic book *The Reflective Practitioner: How Professionals
Think in Action* (1983), Schön similarly argued that thinking and doing
should not be separate; professionals reflect-in-action and react to particular situations as they arise.

Another element that Edgerton, Hutchings, and Quinlan (1991)
stressed is the need to include samples of students' work accompanied by
any feedback from the teacher to the student. Examples of outstanding and
average work might also be included.

From these descriptions, it is clear that the teaching portfolio or dossier goes well beyond what most colleagues have used in the past as a teaching self-report. Typically an annual self-report of activities would include
teaching workload descriptions as well as research and services accomplishments. These annual reports are then the basis for salary and other personnel decisions. Some colleges have extended the guidelines for their
annual self-reports by requesting personal reflections on teaching, examples
of innovations attempted and student course learning, and other specifics.
In other words, self-reports on teaching seem to be becoming more comprehensive, borrowing from the repertoire described for teaching portfolios.
One difference is that the portfolio is supposed to be an ongoing activity,
with entries added throughout the year. Some faculty may view this constant accumulation as busywork and intrusive, as found in one study of
three departments that experimented with portfolio construction and review
(Robinson, 1993). Other two- and four-year colleges have found the portfolio to provide excellent documentation for both formative and summative
purposes (Edgerton, Hutchings, and Quinlan, 1991). And a few graduate
schools, as at Syracuse University, encourage their doctoral students to prepare a teaching portfolio for employment purposes.

Judging Teaching Portfolios or Self-Reports

Judgments of portfolios or self-reports could be made by colleagues, depart-ment chairs, deans, and other administrators. If these judgments are to be used summatively, especially for tenure and promotion purposes, it is important that they be reliable. The rich documentation a portfolio can con-tain provides the basis for making such judgments. Reliability of judgments or ratings, however, is a function not only of the information used but also the number of suitable raters. A single rater, whether an administrator or colleague, provides only a limited view, which can be biased or prejudicial. Additional raters generally provide a more balanced perspective.

Little research has been published on the reliability or validity of col-league or administrator evaluations of course syllabi and other documentary evidence that a teaching portfolio may contain. Most studies have investi-gated colleagues' evaluations of a teacher's overall effectiveness and were based on reputation, hearsay, or other unspecified sources of information. In those studies, colleagues, administrators, and students agreed moderately on their ratings of individual teachers; self-ratings did not, however, corre-late with those made by any other group of raters (Feldman, 1989). Self-evaluations are therefore not a meaningful measure of teaching effectiveness. To the extent that portfolios and self-reports contain self-evaluations or are evaluated by the preparer, they are likely to be less useful in summative deci-sions.

One of the few studies that investigated colleagues' evaluations of teaching dossiers or portfolios was conducted by Root (1987). The dossiers included course outlines, syllabi, teaching materials, student evaluations, and curriculum development documentation—much of what is generally prescribed for a teaching portfolio with the exception of teacher reflections and evidence of student learning. A committee of six elected colleagues independently rated these dossiers after first reviewing and discussing the criteria; cases that illustrated high and low ratings helped clarify the crite-ria. The committee rated research and service as well as teaching, and their ratings were used to determine annual salary increases.

The reliabilities of the evaluations, based on the average intercorrela-tions of the six-member committee, were very high: $-.90$ for each of the three performance areas. In other words, the committee members generally agreed in their evaluations. Root concluded, furthermore, that a three-member committee could provide sufficiently reliable evaluations. Little agreement was found between ratings of research, teaching, and service. Not a reflection on the reliability of the evaluations, this indicated that individu-als who were productive in one area were not necessarily productive in the other two. Other research has also demonstrated that research productivity is not a prerequisite to effective teaching (Centra, 1983; Feldman, 1987).

The Root study supports the use of colleague evaluations of dossier or portfolio materials for tenure and promotion decisions, especially when the committee consists of at least three members and they have previously discussed criteria and standards of performance. How this committee is determined is no doubt also critical. At the institution Root studied, a single elected committee evaluated all faculty dossiers. In a study I conducted at a community college, each teaching portfolio was evaluated by a dean and two peers (Centra, 1994). Teaching effectiveness was described by each faculty member under thirteen categories of performance grouped into three teaching skill areas: motivational skills, interpersonal skills, and intellectual skills. These skill areas and categories were adopted by the college from descriptions of teaching performance provided by Roueche and Baker (1987). Faculty members provided specific examples and descriptions, as well as writing personal statements (reflections) related to their teaching activities. Because this information was to be used to make summative decisions for all ninety-seven faculty members at the college, they took care in preparing their portfolios and included only positive examples.

The individual being evaluated selected one of the peers making portfolio evaluations; area deans selected the second peer. Deans and peers rated only faculty members in their individual areas (divisions). The ratings made by peers selected by individuals being evaluated did not correlate very highly with ratings by the deans or the second peer, nor did those ratings correlate with independently gathered student evaluations of teaching. In contrast, the ratings by the dean and the second peers (named by the dean) correlated positively with each other, as well as with student evaluations of instruction. Thus, it is clear that how colleagues are chosen is critical to the reliability of those colleagues' evaluations. When colleagues are on an ad hoc committee to evaluate a candidate's teaching portfolio and are not being evaluated simultaneously, they can be expected to be somewhat more objective. One college within a research university uses such ad hoc committees to evaluate the teaching effectiveness of faculty members up for tenure or promotion (Centra, 1993). The committee consists of three faculty members and a graduate student, with a senior tenured professor as chair. The faculty member submits material for review, including a personal statement, and the committee also collects information independently (such as ratings by students and alumni). The committee's six-page report is submitted to the tenure and promotion committee to be judged along with research and other criteria. Because a separate committee is named for each faculty member being reviewed, this system does involve considerable faculty time; typically faculty members serve on ad hoc committees every three years and can spend up to forty hours putting together a report on an individual's teaching.

Colleague Evaluations of Portfolios: A Proposal

Portfolios provide an opportunity for faculty members to put forth information on their teaching that cannot be obtained in other ways. For this reason, they should be used in faculty evaluation, especially for summative decisions. But the strength of the portfolio is also part of its weakness: by giving faculty members a chance to make their best case by including positive examples and information, the portfolio does not usually present a balanced view. Certainly some people are better than others at putting a positive spin on their performance.

How then to provide a reliable assessment of the portfolio and also to include balancing information if necessary? Colleagues can and should fill that role. One way they may do this is through an elected colleague committee on teaching. Based on past research, this committee might have as few as three members but certainly no more than six. Their responsibility would be to evaluate the teaching portfolios or self-reports of all faculty members being considered for tenure promotion. Criteria and guidelines would be established for assessing the portfolios and cases that illustrate strong and weak portfolios. The committee members would be expected to obtain their own information if necessary, such as when there is lack of agreement among the committee members in their assessments or inconsistency within the portfolio. The reports by the "Committee on Teaching" would be given to the tenure and promotion committee, as well as to appropriate administrators. At institutions where teaching, research, and service are considered in summative decisions, tenure and promotion committees often do not have the time to make a concerted effort to evaluate teaching portfolios in the way I have described. And at institutions where research is the major, if not the only, criterion in determining tenure and promotion, the "Committees on Teaching" may help give more weight to teaching.

As is generally done with tenure and promotion committees, faculty members might be elected to these teaching committees for brief (two- or three-year) overlapping terms. While the emphasis would be on summative evaluation, it may also be possible to establish a parallel committee for formative evaluation in faculty development. This committee could work in conjunction with personnel in the faculty development office to provide annual or biannual feedback to nontenured faculty members.

Evaluating Teaching: The Future

It is interesting to look back over recent years to note how the evaluation of teaching at the college level has evolved. It is no doubt being evaluated now more than at any time in the past. One of the biggest changes is in the use of student evaluations of teaching. Thirty years ago, student evaluations were used sparingly, and at that were seen largely by the individual professor. I recently came across a 1964 campus newspaper from Michigan State University that contained a debate on the use of student course evaluations. Almost everyone interviewed, especially faculty members and administrators, thought the evaluations should be used only for self-improvement and only at the teacher's discretion. Now student evaluations are used extensively for both formative and summative purposes, often on a mandated basis.

Teaching itself is also evolving. Traditional lecturing, while still dominant, is increasingly being replaced by active learning techniques, including collaborative and cooperative learning, computer-assisted instruction, and other learner-centered approaches. Research continues to demonstrate the effectiveness of active learning in college classrooms, particularly for higher-level learning objectives. This shift in how subject matter is taught will ultimately change how teaching is evaluated. Because the lecture will be limited to a supporting role, it should no longer be the focus of an evaluation. Instead, student learning and the active involvement of students in that learning must be assessed. This can be done in a number of ways.

First, student evaluations of courses and teachers need to change their focus; they should include student assessments of what they have learned in a course, how involved they were in this learning, and how effective the instructional approaches were. Those approaches should include types of active learning as well as the instructor's organization and presentation skills. This change in what students evaluate will alter instruction in desirable ways and will in itself improve student learning. Research has consistently shown the limited value of lengthy lectures in producing student learning, especially long-term learning.

Emphasizing learning rather than teaching (that is, what the instructor does) has recently been promoted as the preferred paradigm. Many factors affect learning, including the student's abilities and effort, as well as the teacher's instructional and motivational techniques (Centra and Gaubatz, 2000). It is extremely difficult to isolate the teacher's contribution to producing course learning. There is, however, no existing template to measure and compare learning gains across a variety of courses. Even comparisons with similar courses or pre- and posttest gains have serious shortcomings, especially if used for summative purposes (Centra 1979, 1993). But although quantity of learning is difficult to judge reliably, quality of learning can more readily be assessed. Quality estimates include the fit between course objectives and the kind of learning assessed in course exams, assignments, and projects. Poor instruction exists when only low-level learning objectives (such as recall of information) are examined, even though the course objectives may include higher-level learning. It can be argued that every course should include such higher-level objectives as application of content, analyses, and critical thinking. Instructional practices should facilitate these outcomes, and they should be reflected in examples of student learning.

Those in the best position to judge quality of learning and instructional practices are well-informed colleagues, and there will be an expanded role for colleagues in the future. This chapter has described how colleagues might best make those judgments. They first need a complete report on instruction and student learning prepared by the individual teacher. Whether called a portfolio, dossier, or something else, these reports must include the array of instructional procedures, outcomes, and reflections that will give colleagues an opportunity to make valid decisions. The instructor's willingness to pull together this evidence and colleagues' willingness to learn how to make valid judgments about teaching are part of what Boyer (1990) described as the scholarship of teaching. That scholarship needs to continue to expand and develop if evaluating teaching and learning in higher education is to improve.

Research has validated the use of student evaluations in helping to judge instructional effectiveness. In the future, we can expect that well-designed studies and development efforts will demonstrate how colleagues can play a larger role in determining faculty effectiveness.

References

Boyer, E. U. *Scholarship Reconsidered: Priorities of the Professorate.* Lawrenceville, N.J.: Princeton University Press, 1990.

Centra, J. A. *Determining Faculty Effectiveness.* San Francisco: Jossey-Bass, 1979.

Centra, J. A. "Research Productivity and Teaching Effectiveness." *Research in Higher Education,* 1983, *18*(2), 379–389.

Centra, J. A. *Reflective Faculty Evaluation: Enhancing Teaching and Determining Faculty Effectiveness.* San Francisco: Jossey-Bass, 1993.

Centra, J. A. "The Use of the Teaching Portfolio and Student Evaluations for Summative Evaluation." *Journal of Higher Education,* 1994, *65*(5).

Centra, J. A., and Gaubatz, N. *Student Perceptions of Learning and Instructional Effectiveness in College Courses, Research Report #9, Higher Education Assessment Program.* Princeton, N.J.: Educational Testing Service, 2000.

Edgerton, R., Hutchings, P., and Quinlan, K. *The Teaching Portfolio: Capturing the Scholarship in Teaching.* Washington, D.C.: American Association for Higher Education, 1991.

Feldman, K. A. "Research Productivity and Scholarly Accomplishments: A Review and Exploration." *Research in Higher Education,* 1987, *26*, 227–298.

Feldman, K. A. "Instructional Effectiveness of College Teachers as Judged by Teachers Themselves, Current and Former Students, Colleagues, Administrators and External (Neutral) Observers." *Research in Higher Education,* 1989, *30*, 137–189.

Robinson, J. "Faculty Orientations Toward Teaching and the Use of Teaching Portfolios for Evaluation and Improving University-Level Instruction." Paper presented at the annual meeting of the American Research Association, Apr. 1993.

Root, L. S. "Faculty Evaluation: Reliability of Peer Assessments of Research, Teaching, and Service." *Research in Higher Education,* 1987, *26*, 71–84.

Roueche, J., and Baker, G. *Access and Excellence: The Open-Door College.* Washington, D.C.: Community College Press, 1987.

Schön, D. *The Reflective Practitioner: How Professionals Think in Action.* New York: Basic Books, 1983.

Shore, B. M., and others. *The Teaching Dossier: A Guide to Its Preparation and Use.* (Rev. ed.) Montreal: Canadian Association of University Teachers, 1986.

Wolf, K. "The Schoolteacher's Portfolio: Practical Issues in Design, Implementation, and Evaluation." *Phi Delta Kappa,* Oct. 1991, pp. 129–136.

JOHN A. CENTRA is professor emeritus of higher education at Syracuse University.

8

Student ratings can be used for several productive purposes, but day-to-day practice often ignores this potential.

Creating Responsive Student Ratings Systems to Improve Evaluation Practice

Michael Theall, Jennifer Franklin

Steadily accumulating evidence of the misuse or overuse of ratings data (Franklin and Theall, 1989) and the perennial debate in the press concerning the validity of student ratings in such publications as the *Chronicle of Higher Education* and *Change* magazine do not invalidate the potential of ratings data as useful information about teaching performance (for example, as established by Centra, 1979, 1993; Marsh, 1987; Theall and Franklin, 1990, 1999b).[1] However, misinformation about ratings and misuse of ratings are closely allied, as our own research demonstrates (Franklin and Theall, 1989). Although articles on the validity and reliability of ratings continue to accumulate in what is arguably the largest single area of research in postsecondary education, the scope of that research has not kept pace with the widespread acceptance of ratings as a measure of teaching effectiveness. Faculty discomfort with ratings and shortfalls in good practice are signs of persistent disjuncture between the worlds of research and practice. Nonetheless, ratings have steadily continued to take precedence in faculty evaluation systems in North America and Australia, are increasingly reported in Asia and Europe, and are attracting considerable attention in the Far East.

To this point, the research literature has been almost exclusively concerned with the construction of ratings instruments. There has been little systematic study of the problem of creating evaluation systems that truly respond to the needs of those who evaluate teaching performance (that of others and their own). A logical first step is to identify and study the wide

New Directions for Teaching and Learning, no. 83, Fall 2000   © Jossey-Bass, a Wiley company

range of contextual variables that actually determine whether ratings are valid, reliable, or usable for the purposes they were intended.

There are two reasons for this suggestion. First, postsecondary education is changing more rapidly than at any time in the past. Recognizing that ratings were first developed during a period when the lecture method ruled and students were far more homogeneous than in today's classrooms, do the assumptions that ground our current view of good practice still hold true? We must continually re-validate and, if needed, revise our approach to be sure that ratings data are valid and reliable in changing contexts, but also to ensure that they are productive and effectively support the decision-making processes they were intended to inform. There are a number of contextual changes to consider:

- Changing instructional practices, such as active, problem-based, and collaborative learning
- Changing student populations, including nontraditional and on-line students
- Changing faculty needs for classroom assessment, formative evaluation, and portfolio development
- Changing institutional priorities for accountability and continuous improvement
- Changing technology and data requirements in on-line instruction and evaluation
- Changing faculty development and evaluation practice, including self and peer evaluation, portfolios, new resources on- and off-campus
- Evolving research perspectives concerning the evaluation context, replication of past research in new settings, and corroboration of findings

A second reason for change is that despite evidence for the validity and reliability of ratings data when acquired with properly constructed and administered instruments, "real-world" ratings practice has not typically been all that good to start with. Ratings have suffered the paradoxical problem of being simultaneously overinterpreted and overrelied on, or being effectively ignored by faculty and faculty evaluators alike in favor of written student comments or other data less appropriate for summative purposes (Franklin and Berman, 1998). The actual day-to-day decisions of those who use ratings are too frequently uninformed by the research literature that professional ratings practitioners hold as their canon.

Practice can certainly be improved by developing the skills and knowledge of the users of ratings (Franklin and Theall, 1999a), but we cannot rest on the assumption that past research can provide all the answers to questions about the evaluation of constantly changing teaching and learning situations. We must study and understand the new dynamics of teaching and learning if we are to evaluate it properly. To this end, we must identify profitable avenues for future research that will help guide the development of new evaluation and ratings techniques.

In this chapter, we discuss what we see as implications of these issues and why we believe consideration of them should be on the agendas of ratings researchers and faculty development practitioners alike. We also point to a systemic problem that has afflicted research and practice from the start, and we offer a tentative draft of a new and expanded agenda for ratings researchers and practitioners, along with some suggestions for improving practice and making student ratings more responsive to the diverse individuals, situations, needs, and complexities of higher education teaching and learning.

Changing Instructional Practices

One practical problem in ratings practice is that current instructional methods are far more varied than the items appearing on commonly used ratings instruments can support. Another problem is the lack of a coherent and widely shared vocabulary to describe current instructional methods. Much of the early ratings research was conducted in traditional classrooms characterized by relatively restricted teaching methods such as lectures, seminars, and discussion groups. Even then there were many exceptions to the lecture—for example, labs, studios, clinical work, practicums, programmed instruction, and individual study courses. However, attempts to consider the generalizability of ratings items to various instructional settings can be confounded by the lack of clear definition of teaching methods versus course formats.

As new teaching techniques such as those designed to foster active or collaborative learning (Johnson, Johnson, and Smith, 1991) became more widely adopted, the same standard forms were often used, raising important questions about the validity and utility of ratings as a source of data for formative or summative evaluation. Use of standard forms outside the contexts within which they were developed is founded on the unproven assumption that "one size fits all." This argument may be made for very short forms with global items asking very general question concerning the course and the teacher, but the more specific a ratings form is in terms of teacher behaviors or course components, the more likely it is to contain items that do not apply in the same way in the new setting, if at all. Setting aside the validity question, that is, which items do not work (or work differently) outside the lecture context, it should be obvious that absent items directly related to the instructional method being used, ratings data cannot deliver adequately detailed feedback for teaching improvement purposes. Distance and asynchronous learning present situations even further removed from those used to establish both the psychometric properties and practical applications of ratings data. We would venture to guess that by now, every manager of a campus ratings system has been contacted by someone requesting ratings for a Web-based course. What are "teacher behaviors" in such a setting? Who or what is different when the presentation of course content and assessment of student learning are managed by a computer, and what behaviors or outcomes are benchmarks of successful performance?

To address the problem of instructional variability, several well-known ratings systems (such as the Purdue Cafeteria system, the University of Illinois Multi-Op–ICES system, and our own Teacher-Course Evaluation system) offer banks of items related to specialized situations such as lab and studio instruction, as well as the now traditional teacher behavior and course items. To the degree that items are available to match faculty interest, recent developments in computing technology have made delivery of such services much more practical. For example, it is now possible to allow faculty to customize their own forms via the Web cost-effectively. There is a caution, however. Expanded access to such services does not guarantee that ratings will in fact lead to improved instruction. Some evidence exists to suggest that some faculty are not able to select appropriate items (Ory and Weities, 1991). Moreover, there is a natural tendency to select items that will produce higher ratings when those ratings are used for summative performance appraisal.

Although "specialty" items are typically developed on an ad hoc, face-valid basis with little or no systematic validation, they have generally been constructed by practitioners with some training in survey item construction. This is an important point, because to the casual faculty observer accustomed to taking polls and surveys, it may seem very simple to write items and only a technicality to use new technologies such as feedback forms on a course Web site to administer them. Our experience providing evaluation services and consulting to individuals and institutions suggests that the proliferation of faculty committee–made questionnaires stems from just such a confidence. Unfortunately, much more than confidence and superficial face validity are required for reliable and valid evaluation. All the major commercial and institutional forms have undergone extensive analysis of their psychometric properties as well as extensive use in the field with subsequent reanalysis of their results. Even subsets of questions (for example, Murray's work on the development of "low inference" teacher behaviors in 1983 and 1997) have been subject to lengthy series of research studies.

Changing Student Populations

Changing student populations bring the question of generalizability of ratings results back in to the foreground. Increases in the number of nontraditional students raise issues about the applicability of earlier research drawn largely from a residential population of students eighteen to twenty-one years old. Adult learners are frequently characterized as more responsible, more motivated, and possessing other characteristics that likely influence their expectations of their teachers and, in turn, what determines their satisfaction with the instruction they receive. The influx of international students to the United States and Canada has brought more and more students who began their education in other cultures and then entered North American postsecondary institutions. Those who work with international graduate teaching assistants are familiar with complaints concerning the attitudes and work habits of undergraduate students or those students' lack of respect for their teachers. The steady increase in the numbers of female students and the proportionate decrease in the numbers of male students may signal the need to revisit norms built on long-standing databases drawn from student populations with different demographics.

Shifts in student ethnicity demographics raise other questions. Cultural differences in student perceptions of effective teaching impose severe methodological problems in a system that relies on student anonymity. Thus, few data have been acquired concerning the impact of this variable. Yet what may be very effective teaching for one group of students may be less optimal for others, depending on culturally determined learning styles or preferences of students. In some areas of the United States, increases in immigrant populations have substantially changed the ethnic makeup of public postsecondary classrooms. A recent study finding notable differences in the ratings given by international students from different cultural groups to teachers of English as a second language (Franklin and Theall, 1999b) signals the need for more investigation of this phenomenon.

Changing Faculty Needs: Classroom Assessment, Formative Evaluation, and Portfolio Development

During the same period that ratings were taking hold, the community of faculty development practitioners expanded their repertoire of strategies for collecting student feedback for the purpose of helping their clients improve their teaching skills or courses. The use of focus group methods in the classroom (SGID: small group instructional diagnosis), the rise of the classroom assessment movement, and other structured methods for learning what students think about their classes and teachers (for example, "minute papers" and other techniques described by Angelo and Cross, 1993) contributed to an emerging redefinition of the role of student-provided data (including ratings) as source material for teaching improvement. Some faculty developers use this variety of data sources extensively, while some with more limited interests or skill focus on only qualitative or quantitative data. This is unfortunate because a complete understanding of teaching and learning situations requires both kinds of information from students, teachers, and other sources. In fairness, however, it must be said that instructional consultants often must work with whatever data are available. In many institutions, ratings data are regarded with suspicion. Poor practice invalidates the use of ratings data even for formative purposes, and the only useful tools available to consultants are those qualitative methods that do not rely on the analysis of data from ratings questionnaires.

The widespread interest in dossiers (Shore and others, 1986) and portfolios (Seldin, 1991) has also had an impact on evaluation practice. Typical portfolio materials include items such as self-evaluations, written student comments, statements of teaching-learning philosophies, peer evaluations, and the results of qualitative explorations of classroom process. These are appealing to faculty because they offer alternatives to the more traditional (and often less favored) kinds of quantitative data provided by student ratings. Although the interpretation and use of ratings data have been shown to be a problem area (Franklin and Theall, 1989), the use of typical portfolio items may present even greater problems because few, if any, guidelines for their interpretation and use exist. For example, although there are at least some generally accepted guidelines for adequate sample size in course ratings (Theall and Franklin, 1991b), there are no similar guidelines for student comments, self-evaluations, and other data. Centra (1994) and Robinson (1993) have both reported faculty concerns about this issue and noted the reliability problems associated with using these kinds of data.

In sum, ratings and other evaluation data must be responsive to the needs of the individual and the institution. This is one of Miller's (1986) ten characteristics of effective systems and a principle embedded in the most recent attempts to develop comprehensive evaluation systems (Arreola, 1995). However, this responsiveness requires both a wide array of data and adequate processes for analyzing, reporting, and interpreting those data. It is in this arena that evaluation practice suffers its greatest lack of precision.

Changing Institutional Priorities: Accountability and Continuous Improvement

The advent of Total Quality Management and related practices in higher education has resulted in many institutions' using student ratings data as measures of satisfaction or as student learning outcomes indicators in institutional reports to governing bodies. These reports cannot be long or overly technical. The conundrum is that these external users of evaluation data are likely to be the least sophisticated in interpreting and using ratings. They need to understand the underlying meaning of the numbers that are presented because their decisions affect the whole higher education community. Judging institutional effectiveness by comparing average ratings would be a serious error, for example. This public use of the data also means that ratings systems should be designed to capture data from those contextual variables that must be tracked to help explain or control sources of systemic variation. How student, teacher, and course characteristics are described in a ratings system will determine the quality of the questions that may be asked of the ratings data in institutional research on the quality of instruction and student satisfaction. At minimum, ratings systems should be designed or selected with consultation from persons trained in college teaching and learning, instructional design, evaluation practice, and database management, who can advise ratings systems operators on the design, maintenance, and use of institutional ratings systems. Equally important as a minimum standard should be the presentation of information in ways that maximize effective and accurate decision making (Franklin and Theall, 1990).

Changing Technology and Data Requirements

Just as in the world at large, advances in technology can simultaneously improve or worsen current practice. Decreases in the cost of optical mark read technology and user-friendly Web authoring systems for collecting feedback using the Internet mean that relatively little expertise is required to collect ratings data. Anyone can create and scan a questionnaire or administer it on-line. However, collecting end-of-semester ratings data cost-effectively, accurately, and in a timely manner is best done by ensuring that qualified data processing technicians maintain the system under the supervision of someone knowledgeable about the ratings and their uses and limitations. It is a paradox that the quality of ratings practice in an institution can be undermined by access to the very technology that makes it possible for qualified practitioners to improve the quality and scope of the services they offer.

It can be argued that, setting technology aside, there is little coherence in the ways in which we identify new methods or strategies. Even if more items reflecting current instructional practices were available, there is disagreement concerning the meaning of widely used terms such as *collaborative* and *cooperative* learning strategies. Another example is the widespread confounding of terms such as *teaching styles, learning styles,* and *teaching methods.* While it may be useful to know that a teacher is an "accommodator" or a student is a "diverger" in one typology, the question is whether such knowledge can be put to good use in improving teaching and learning. With respect to our discussion in this chapter, the next question must be, How can we (if at all) use such knowledge to assess teaching performance accurately?

This issue is symptomatic of the failure of researchers to establish and share a coherent vocabulary for postsecondary instructional phenomena in general. However, discourse among researchers fuels the proliferation of new terminology and jargon that trickles down to higher education practitioners in ways that rarely carry forward the theoretical context that informs the terms and ensures that they are used reliably or meaningfully. Good evaluation practice must include an understanding of relevant theory and avoid misuse of those principles and terms that have been established and tested.

The rapid growth of distance education, particularly asynchronous and on-line teaching and learning, is a major new issue in evaluation. Literally everyone involved in the uses of new technologies for teaching and learning acknowledges that the contexts and situations of on-line learning are substantially different from those in face-to-face instruction. Yet despite this realization, many on-line programs simply adopt the process and instruments used in traditional courses. Student ratings collected with these instruments do not address the unique characteristics of the on-line teaching-learning situation and thus do not provide data specific enough to allow accurate understanding of the outcomes of instruction. How, then, can data from these instruments be used to make decisions that rely on the comparison of faculty ratings from different contexts? At an even more fundamental level, we must admit that what we know about college teaching and learning has been derived largely from populations of younger, residential students in traditional classes, and in some cases, the courses on which the research was based were predominantly entry-level, large-enrollment courses. Although the extrapolation of results from the traditional context to on-line teaching and learning situations is not totally unwarranted, replication of the research in the new situations is needed before we can say with assurance that the same findings hold. Given this and the lackluster history of research comparing on-line and traditional instruction (Russell, 1999), it would be difficult at this time to point to definitive findings that could guide the evaluation of on-line teaching. A simple but clear example of our lack of guidelines is the question of the impact of the technology itself on ratings. We do not know whether students enter classes with positive or negative views and value systems regarding technology or the experience they are about to embark on. We do not know whether on-line dialogue is comparable to face-to-face dialogue. We do not know whether the sense of community established in a successful campus classroom can be replicated (or duplicated, matched, equaled, copied, or improved) on-line. Perhaps most obvious, we do not know the extent to which the technical performance of the systems used in on-line teaching and learning affects student and teacher behaviors, efforts, attitudes, and outcomes.

Some methods for assessing the success of on-line and distance education have been proposed (Chickering and Ehrmann, 1997), but questions have been raised (Neal, 1998) about the extent to which such processes omit consideration of the outcomes of instruction. The situation today is precarious because sound evaluation practices are required, but we do not have the research base on which to base decisions about practice. Clearly, much more investigation is required before we can claim understanding of these new situations equal to that we now hold about traditional college teaching and learning.

Changing Faculty Development and Evaluation Practices

The term *faculty development* has many definitions, perhaps as many as there are individuals involved, and these range from interest in personal growth and spiritual wellness, to a desire for complete autonomy in establishing one's own agenda, to financial support for traditional benefits such as travel to conferences, to simple opportunities to discuss teaching and one's discipline. Our main concern here is with the use of evaluation data for faculty development. Experience and research show that it is not enough to hand out ratings data. Users vary widely in their need for support in interpreting those data, and more support results in more improvement (Cohen, 1980; Menges and Brinko, 1986).

It is not merely a question of interpreting numbers. Understanding how ratings relate to effective teaching requires someone with a wider range of skills than either a statistician or even an expert teacher may possess. The task of interpreting ratings also varies by purpose. The skills that a teacher needs to use ratings in the context of reflective practice are quite different from the performance appraisal skills that a department head needs to review ratings or that a committee needs in negotiating their sometimes conflicting interpretations of ratings and student-written comments. Although there are a number of sources offering guides or tips on the subject, there has been little systematic study of what works best and what does not work at all. Systematic examination of even anecdotal evidence would be helpful. The generalizations such as those offered based on our experience still need grounding with data.

Productively exploring ratings in a way that helps an individual improve his or her teaching skills also requires consulting skills, which include skills more often found in counseling. However, as a practical matter, there will never be enough staff resources to explain ratings personally to everyone who could benefit from the explanation. That means that other strategies such as workshops and printed and on-line guides to interpreting ratings are also needed. Skills can be improved, as recent research (Franklin and Theall, 1999a) has shown. But perhaps more important even than skill is the larger picture of the reward structures, politics, and practices at the institutional level. Even the best data can be misused. Even the best data collection, analysis, and reporting system can be subverted. Even the best teaching can be ignored in favor of some other aspect of performance. Good evaluation requires the definition of the characteristics and performance to be considered and the commitment of institutions and the individuals within them to use the best possible evidence accurately and fairly to make decisions.

Evaluation and development, then, are inextricably connected. They can stand alone, but each becomes much more productive in the presence of the other. Perhaps the greatest need in evaluation and development practice is to solidify this position and establish the productive uses of evaluation and ratings as connected to improvement and positive change. Unfortunately, the reverse has often been the case, and evaluation has been considered a punitive process. As the previous paragraph suggests, good practice requires an institutional commitment to move in the positive direction and to support the best uses of evaluation data for growth and improvement.

Changing Research Perspectives

In the past fifteen years, the emphasis of the literature on student ratings has begun to turn from largely psychometric issues to discussions about the quality and adequacy of evaluation practice. After Marsh's (1987) definitive review of past research and restatement of the general validity and reliability of ratings, many investigators turned toward the exploration and improvement of practice (for example our own work in Franklin and Theall, 1989; Theall and Franklin, 1990). With this change came the realization that reliance on ratings alone was insufficient for good practice, and this led to thinking about new ways of documenting performance (for example, dossiers in Shore and others, 1986, and portfolios in Seldin, 1991), as well as the development of processes and methods leading to more comprehensive evaluation systems (Arreola, 1995; Theall, Franklin, and Birdsall, 1987).

With the nearly four decades of research on sources of systematic variation in ratings, the relationship between ratings and variables such as rank, class size, gender, and course level has been relatively well established. More recently issues such as disciplinary differences (Hativa and Marincovich, 1995), instructional design factors (Franklin and Theall, 1992), perceptions of the value of course components and activities (Franklin and Theall, 1995), and the effect of context (Feldman, 1998) have emerged as new factors in understanding and using ratings effectively. However, these and other studies also illustrate the problem of a lack of a common vocabulary to describe such factors reliably.

Having a more coherent typology to describe the characteristics and behaviors of postsecondary teachers and learners and their interactions would seem a logical foundation for the evaluation of postsecondary teaching and teachers. Thus, we are increasingly concerned with two important areas that are logically related to good practice in the measurement of instructional quality, and which remain largely unstudied:

The generalizability of typical ratings items as described in the literature to the wide range of new instructional modes and pedagogical methods, particularly when those modes and methods are themselves inconsistently described

The organizational infrastructure and professional and staff resources needed to create (or adopt), maintain, and productively use a well-crafted ratings system within an institution

A third area resides in the nexus of the previous two: having a reliable and extensive common vocabulary to describe important postsecondary phenomena is essential to any valid generalizing of ratings findings, and that also means having an appropriately trained staff to administer the system to collect ratings data and provide support to those who use the data.

Conclusion

The evaluation of faculty performance, and indeed, of program, school, and institutional performance, requires the investment of time, resources, thought, and goodwill. True systems for evaluation include technical and mechanical components, to be sure. They also require skilled practitioners and dedicated faculty, administrators, and students. Because incomplete or inaccurate systems have the potential to do more harm' than good, it is critical that the entire system be valid, reliable, accurate, efficient, and accepted. Only then will the one component of student ratings be able to provide its unique part of the overall picture, an accurate record of the impressions and reactions of those for whom the entire higher education enterprise was established: the students we are committed to teach, the graduates who will later judge the value of their experiences, and the citizens who will determine the future of higher education.

Note

1. In 1998, the *Chronicle of Higher Education* published an article entitled, "New Research Casts Doubt on Value of Student Evaluations of Professors" (January 16). The article presented a strongly canted view that ratings are invalid. A subsequent discussion took place in an on-line *Chronicle* discussion area called "Colloquy" [then at http:/chronicle.com /colloquy/98/evaluation/X.htm, where "X" was the sequence number of the response]. These responses were reviewed by Theall in "Colloquy: An Editorial," *Instructional Development and Faculty Evaluation,* 18 (1–2) [http://www.uis.edu/~ctl/sigfed/backissue.html]. The negative responses were characterized by a display of a lack of knowledge of the evaluation literature and an excessive reliance on personal opinion and anecdote.

The September–October 1997 issue of *Change* magazine published two articles critical of student ratings. The articles were harshly criticized by evaluation researchers for their methodological weaknesses, lack of generalizability, and failure to demonstrate that changes in ratings were due to the supposed causes: artificial changes in teacher behavior and greater teacher leniency. Nonetheless, these articles were frequently cited as "evidence" that ratings data are invalid.

References

Angelo, T. A., and Cross, K. P. *Classroom Assessment Techniques: A Handbook for College Teachers.* (2nd ed.) San Francisco: Jossey-Bass, 1993.

Arreola, R. A. *Developing a Comprehensive Faculty Evaluation System.* Bolton, Mass.: Anker Publications, 1995.

Brinko, K. T., and Menges, R. J. *Practically Speaking: A Source Book for Instructional Consultants in Higher Education.* Stillwater, Okla.: New Forums Press, 1997.

Centra, J. A. *Determining Faculty Effectiveness: Assessing Teaching, Research, and Service for Personnel Decisions and Improvement.* San Francisco: Jossey-Bass, 1979.

Centra, J. A. (1993) *Reflective Faculty Evaluation.* San Francisco: Jossey-Bass, 1993.

Centra, J. A. "The Use of the Teaching Portfolio and Student Evaluations for Summative Evaluation." *Journal of Higher Education,* 1994, 65(5), 555–570.

Chickering, A. W., and Ehrmann, S. C. "Implementing the Seven Principles: Technology as Lever." American Association for Higher Education. [http://www.tltgroup.org /programs/seven.html]. 1997.

Cohen, P. A. "Effectiveness of Student Ratings Feedback for Improving College Instruction: A Meta-Analysis of Findings." *Research in Higher Education,* 1980, *13*(4), 321–341.

Cohen, P. A. "Student Ratings of Instruction and Student Achievement: A Meta-Analysis of Multisection Validity Studies." *Review of Educational Research,* 1981, *31*(3), 281–309.

Feldman, K. A. "Reflections on the Effective Study of College Teaching and Student Ratings: One Continuing Quest and Two Unresolved Issues." In J. C. Smart (ed.), *Higher Education: Handbook of Theory and Research.* New York: Agathon Press, 1998.

Franklin, J., and Berman, E. "Using Student Written Comments in Evaluating Teaching." *Instructional Evaluation and Faculty Development,* 1998, *18*(1). [http://www.uis.edu/~ctl/sigfed/backissues.html].

Franklin, J., and Theall, M. "Who Reads Ratings: Knowledge, Attitudes, and Practices of Users of Student Ratings of Instruction." Paper presented at the Seventieth Annual Meeting of the American Educational Research Association, San Francisco, 1989. (ED 30 62 41)

Franklin, J., and Theall, M. "Communicating Student Ratings Results to Decision Makers; Design for Good Practice." In M. Theall and J. Franklin (eds.), *Effective Practices for Improving Teaching.* New Directions for Teaching and Learning, no. 48. San Francisco: Jossey-Bass, 1990.

Franklin, J., and Theall, M. "Disciplinary Differences, Instructional Goals and Activities, Measures of Student Performance, and Student Ratings of Instruction." Paper presented at the Seventy-Third Annual Meeting of the American Educational Research Association, San Francisco, 1992.

Franklin, J., and Theall, M. "The Relationship of Disciplinary Differences and the Value of Class Preparation Time to Student Ratings of Instruction." In N. Hativa and M. Marincovich (eds.), *Disciplinary Differences in Teaching and Learning: Implications for Practice.* New Directions for Teaching and Learning, no. 64. San Francisco: Jossey-Bass, 1995.

Franklin, J., and Theall, M. "Thinking About Faculty Thinking About Teacher and Course Evaluation Results." Paper presented at the Seventy-Second Annual Meeting of the American Educational Research Association, Montreal, 1999a.

Franklin, J., and Theall, M. "Regional/Cultural Differences in the TCE Responses of International Students in an American ESL Program." Paper presented at the Eightieth Annual Meeting of the American Educational Research Association, Montreal, 1999b.

Hativa, N., and Marincovich, M. (eds.). *Disciplinary Differences in Teaching and Learning: Implications for Practice.* New Directions for Teaching and Learning, no. 64. San Francisco: Jossey-Bass, 1995.

Johnson, D. W., Johnson, R. T., and Smith, K. A. *Cooperative Learning: Increasing College Faculty Productivity.* Washington, D.C.: George Washington University, 1991.

Marsh, H. W. "Student Evaluations of University Teaching: Research Findings, Methodological Issues, and Directions for Future Research." *International Journal of Educational Research,* 1987, *11,* 253–388.

Menges, R. J., and Brinko, K. T. "Effects of Student Evaluation Feedback: A Meta-Analysis of Higher Education Research." Paper presented at the Seventieth Annual Meeting of the American Educational Research Association, San Francisco, 1986. (ED 270 408)

Miller, R. I. *Evaluating Faculty for Promotion and Tenure.* San Francisco: Jossey-Bass, 1986.

Murray, H. G. "Low-Inference Classroom Teaching Behaviors and Student Ratings of College Teaching Effectiveness." *Journal of Educational Psychology,* 1983, *75*(1), 138–149.

Murray, H. G. "Effective Teaching Behaviors in the College Classroom." In J. C. Smart (ed.), *Higher Education Handbook of Theory and Research.* New York: Agathon, 1997.

Neal, E. "Does Using Technology in Instruction Enhance Learning? or, the Artless State of Comparative Research." *Technological Horizons in Education Journal Commentary,* 1998. [http://horizon.unc.edu/TS/commentary/1998–06.asp].

Ory, J. C., and Weities, R. "A Longitudinal Study of Faculty Selection of ICES Student Evaluation Items." Paper presented at the Seventy-Second Annual Meeting of the American Educational Research Association, Chicago, 1991.

Robinson, J. "Faculty Orientations Toward Teaching and the Use of Teaching Portfolios for Evaluating and Improving University-Level Instruction." Paper presented at the Seventy-Fourth Annual Meeting of the American Educational Research Association, Atlanta, 1993.

Russell, T. L. *The No Significant Difference Phenomenon.* Raleigh: North Carolina State University, 1999.

Seldin, P. *The Teaching Portfolio: A Practical Guide to Improved Performance and Promotion/Tenure Decisions.* Bolton Mass.: Anker Publications, 1991.

Shore, B. M., and others. *The Teaching Dossier: A Guide to Its Preparation and Use.* Ottawa: Canadian Association of University Professors, 1986.

Theall, M., and Franklin, J. (eds.). *Student Ratings of Instruction: Issues for Improving Practice.* New Directions for Teaching and Learning, no. 43. San Francisco: Jossey-Bass, 1990.

Theall, M., and Franklin, J. (eds.). *Effective Practices for Improving Teaching.* New Directions for Teaching and Learning, no. 48. San Francisco: Jossey-Bass, 1991a.

Theall, M., and Franklin, J. Using Student Ratings for Teaching Improvement. In M. Theall and J. Franklin (eds.), *Effective Practices for Improving Teaching.* New Directions for Teaching and Learning, no. 48. San Francisco: Jossey-Bass, 1991b.

Theall, M., Franklin, J., and Birdsall, M. "The Development of a Computer-Based, Diagnostic-Prescriptive System for Evaluation and Teaching Improvement." Paper presented at the Second National Conference on Faculty Evaluation and Development, Orlando, Fla., 1987.

MICHAEL THEALL *is associate professor of educational leadership and director of the Center for Teaching and Learning at the University of Illinois at Springfield.*

JENNIFER FRANKLIN *is director of the Center for Teaching and Learning at California State University at Dominguez Hills.*

9

This chapter examines key issues from the evaluation-of-teaching literature; the authors suggest a multifaceted approach to the evaluation of college teaching.

A Comprehensive Approach to the Evaluation of College Teaching

Trav D. Johnson, Katherine E. Ryan

The literature on the evaluation of college teaching is rich and varied, ranging from general work on developing effective faculty evaluations to very specific research investigating a variety of methods for evaluating teaching, such as student ratings, peer observation, and portfolios (Braskamp and Ory, 1994, Cambridge, 1996; Centra, 1993; Morehead and Shedd, 1996; Seldin, 1997). However, there is no real consensus on how to evaluate teaching in higher education. There continues to be a fundamental tension in addressing college teaching evaluation from a personnel perspective and a developmental perspective while simultaneously dealing with institutional goals. The task is complicated by an increasing recognition of differing teaching evaluation situations, each with its own set of characteristics and needs. In addition, further research and understanding are needed in critical areas that inform the evaluation and improvement of teaching.

Our purposes in this chapter are to identify some of the most pressing issues or needs in improving the evaluation of college teaching, discuss the implications of these issues and how they may be addressed in practice, and provide a brief description of what a comprehensive evaluation system designed to address these issues and implications may look like.

Issues at the Heart of the Conversation

A review of current literature reveals four issues that seem to be at the heart of improving the evaluation of college teaching: defining faculty roles and expectations, understanding teachers and teaching contexts, meeting the

New Directions for Teaching and Learning, no. 83, Fall 2000 © Jossey-Bass, a Wiley company

multiple demands placed on teaching evaluations, and the need for better use of evaluation in faculty development.

Defining Faculty Roles and Expectations. One of the most fundamental challenges facing the evaluation of college teaching is defining specific expectations of faculty in regard to teaching. Kumaravadivelu (1995) describes teaching effectiveness as an "elusive concept" that is challenging to define and even harder to assess. Cavanagh (1996) points out the common concern that "there is no consensus about what constitutes effective teaching" (p. 237). Yet as Richlin and Manning (1996) explain, this understanding is critical to effective teaching evaluation. Hutchings (1996) believes that in addition to reaching a better understanding of what it means to be an effective teacher, we must come to some agreement about what constitutes significant student learning. Others (Boggs, 1999; Cambridge, 1996; Ellett and others, 1997) also see a need to focus more on student learning in the evaluation of teaching.

This lack of agreement may be fueled in part by changing definitions of teaching and learning. Centra (1993) describes changes in American education, including a recent call for more active learning. Braskamp and Ory (1994) also see shifts in this direction:

> At all educational levels, teaching is now being viewed more broadly. Didactic teaching—where the teacher is the master and the students the disciples— is no longer the norm. The roles of teachers and students are changing as greater collaboration between students and instructors is now being stressed. Students are to be active and engaged learners rather than passive recipients [p. 39].

Braskamp (Chapter Three, this volume) adds to the discussion by contrasting two views of faculty teaching roles—one role emphasizing student learning and the other emphasizing teacher development. Others have described faculty roles similarly, either emphasizing the "student leaning paradigm" (Boggs, 1999) or focusing on the development of individual faculty members (Palmer, 1998) as the key to improving teaching and learning. Although these two faculty roles are not mutually exclusive, they do represent very different views with alternative implications to teaching and its evaluation. Braskamp contends that a clear understanding of the faculty teaching role in relation to these (or other) conceptions of teaching is a critical element of good evaluation practice.

Implications. Many believe that a key to defining faculty roles and expectations is the clarification of institution and unit goals in regard to teaching and learning (Braskamp and Ory, 1994; Cashin, 1996; Cavanagh, 1996; Gray, Adam, Froh, and Yonai, 1994). Clearly identified goals and expectations can provide the basis for establishing evaluation criteria, which make effective teaching evaluation possible (Cashin, 1996). Institutional goals are important in establishing general evaluation criteria. These goals may be identified in a number of ways, including the examination of official documents (such as mission statements, policy speeches) and working with campus leadership to clarify specific purposes and responsibilities regarding faculty roles (Gray and Diamond, 1994). Unit and instructor goals guide the development of specific evaluation criteria. These criteria may be developed through in-depth discussion among colleagues in a particular department or unit (Cavanagh, 1996; Richlin and Manning, 1995).

Defining expectations of faculty in relation to institutional and unit goals will require ongoing efforts by faculty and administrators to identify clearly and also gain general support for the expectations that are decided on. Because of the variety of contexts in which teaching occurs, these expectations will necessarily be institution, department, and to some extent instructor and course specific. In most cases, this will require considerable inquiry, dialogue, reflection, and reference to the literature on teaching. Faculty input and participation will be central to the process. This is not an easy task, but it is nevertheless essential. Understanding the roles and expectations of instructors in regard to teaching and learning is a central issue in establishing evaluation criteria, determining appropriate use of evaluation results, developing evaluations that are of optimum use in faculty development, and aligning evaluation and development efforts with department and institutional goals.

In addition to defining faculty roles and expectations, it will be helpful for departments and institutions to focus general evaluation and development efforts on areas that are common to a variety of faculty roles and expectations. For example, Braskamp (Chapter Three, this volume) points out that learning communities are important to both of the faculty roles he contrasts. Stake and Cisneros-Cohernour (Chapter Five, this volume) emphasize a similar concept in their discussion of communities of practice. Therefore, efforts to develop learning communities or communities of practice are likely to enhance evaluation and development efforts for many instructors and departments regardless of the different faculty roles and expectations they emphasize. One way to encourage learning communities and communities of practice is the development of department and institutional cultures that view teaching as "community property" that is shared, discussed, and evaluated within a community of scholars (Shulman, 1993). This type of culture may be encouraged through various collaborative efforts aimed at understanding and improving teaching, such as peer coaching and mentoring (Harnish and Wild, 1994; Skinner and Welch, 1996), horizontal teacher evaluation (Gitlin and Goldstein, 1987), and teaching circles (Bernstein, 1996).

Another strategy for dealing with different faculty roles and expectations is the use of multiple evaluation criteria. Through the use of multiple criteria, evaluations can provide information on different aspects of teaching and instructional improvement that are emphasized in different faculty roles and expectations. For example, evaluation criteria might include measures of student learning, assessment of teaching methods and materials, information on faculty self-understanding and development, and measures of faculty contributions to instructional improvement within a department or institution. By employing multiple criteria such as these, an evaluation effort can yield information that is useful to faculty in varying roles and to evaluation audiences that focus on different expectations.

Understanding Teachers and Teaching Contexts. A second important area of the evaluation of teaching is understanding teachers and the contexts in which teaching and evaluation occur. Menges (Chapter One, this volume) addresses the underlying aspects of teaching and how instructors use evaluative information to improve their practice. He points out the need to understand why faculty teach as they do, how they interpret and use evaluative information, how their personal theories about teaching and learning are developed, and the relationship between their internal perceptions and external behaviors. Braskamp and Ory (1994) ask that we examine faculty members' goals and the thinking behind their work. Similarly, Pratt (1997) describes the need for a more substantive (rather than technical) approach to evaluating teaching that includes a focus on instructor intentions and beliefs.

Many authors recognize the importance of understanding teaching contexts in the evaluation of teaching (Angelo, 1996; Braskamp and Ory, 1994; Kahn, 1993; McKeachie, 1996; Murray, 1995; Neumann, 1994; Richlin and Manning, 1996). Angelo (1996) states, "Assessing and evaluating teaching effectively requires knowledge of and a sensitivity to the individuals and groups involved, the local context, and the academic and administrative culture of the institution" (p. 62). Stake (1987) explains it this way:

> An effective evaluation of teaching requires concurrent study of institutional goals, classroom environments, administrative organization and operations, curricular content, student achievement, and the impact of programs on state and society. Teaching can be judged properly only in the context of these and other factors—and if no effort is made to study them, the evaluation of teaching probably will be invalid [p. 1].

Shulman (1993) emphasizes the importance of discipline differences in teaching. He argues for reconnecting teaching and its evaluation to the disciplines, including discipline-specific evaluations of teaching. In research on the evaluation of teaching in different disciplines, Quinlan (1995) found clear differences in a variety of areas of teaching and learning between chemistry and history departments. McKeachie (1996) points out the pitfalls of trying to compare teachers teaching in different departments at different class levels with different students. He argues that this is neither necessary nor desirable in the evaluation of teaching.

Implications. Recognizing the importance of understanding teachers and teaching contexts leads to a number of implications for the evaluation of teaching. Among these is the need to use evaluation methods and sources that are most likely to provide information in these areas. Qualitative methods (such as focus groups, interviews, and observations) are especially useful in providing data on the thought processes and motivations of teachers and the contexts in which they teach. Information on teachers and teaching contexts may also come from analysis of documents or records such as personal and departmental goal statements, teacher logs or journals, and course, department, and college demographic information. Portfolios are a useful way to compile information and capture the complexities of teaching and teaching contexts (Richlin and Manning, 1996; Smith, 1995). Sources that are valuable in providing teacher and contextual information include administrators, students, peers, and instructors. These sources can provide multiple perspectives of teachers and the courses, departments, and institutions in which they teach.

To incorporate these methods and sources into the evaluation of teaching, those involved will need to move beyond using only student ratings of instruction and become more comfortable with different forms and sources of information. Understanding and using qualitative data will be especially important. In addition, practitioners will need to change the way they interpret evaluation results. Instead of making broad comparisons among faculty using single numeric measures of teaching, interpretations will rely more on understanding teachers and how well teaching meets context-specific goals and needs. Defining and understanding the context will be essential in designing evaluations and understanding and interpreting evaluation results.

In an effort to understand teachers and teaching contexts, it will be helpful to determine the needs and goals of specific instructors, students, departments, and institutions. This will require that those involved in the teaching-learning process identify and articulate their needs and goals. For some individuals, departments, and institutions that have already made strides in this area, this task may be relatively easy. For others it will require considerable inquiry, reflection, and dialogue to understand their own and others' perspectives and determine needs and goals that are most important. This will take more effort at the front end of evaluations to identify and incorporate needs and goals into the overall evaluation process.

Those involved in the evaluation of teaching will also need to consider how evaluation results are used in specific contexts. For example, in departments that have a large percentage of faculty members team-teaching or in teaching rotations, evaluations may be used primarily at the department level to assess and improve collaboration among instructors and the organization and delivery of the curriculum. If a faculty member is being considered for tenure, evaluations will focus on the overall quality of instruction and the match between the instructor's contributions and college and departmental needs. In some institutions, teaching evaluations may be used extensively; in others they may be used very little. Since use is an important goal of evaluation (Patton, 1997), understanding how results are used and how they can best be used in a given context is essential. Evaluations should be designed to facilitate optimum use and decision making in each context. Those designing evaluations may also work to alter evaluation contexts to make them more conducive to increased and appropriate use of evaluation results. These aims can be accomplished by understanding context-specific needs and goals and involving primary stakeholders in designing the evaluation.

Involving stakeholders such as faculty, administrators, and students in evaluation design is one of the best ways to improve use (Higgerson, 1999; Patton, 1997; Ryan and Johnson, 2000) and tailor evaluations to specific contexts. In other evaluation situations, this involvement has increased the likelihood that evaluation results are used by helping stakeholders to have ownership in the evaluation process (Cousins and Earl, 1995; Ryan, Geissler, and Knell, 1996). It also provides an opportunity to educate participants in the appropriate use of results and how to incorporate evaluation results in local decision making. There are multiple ways in which faculty can be included in making decisions about how to evaluate teaching. One approach is conducting focus groups with faculty or holding campus-level public meetings to determine what kinds of teaching evaluation information are most useful to faculty. Once this information is obtained, it can be incorporated into the teaching evaluation system. Another way to include faculty directly in the evaluation process is convening faculty committees to review and make recommendations regarding current teaching evaluation practices.

Multiple Demands on Teaching Evaluations. Increasing demands on teaching evaluations include pressures from both inside and outside institutions of higher learning. Pressures from the outside are requiring increased accountability and demonstrations of effectiveness:

> Legislatures, boards of trustees, parents, the media, various academic disciplines and professional associations, and accrediting organizations are calling on higher education to demonstrate greater responsiveness to an increasingly diverse student body and the increasingly acute problems of society. At the same time, demands are being made that higher education become more efficient and effective in its use of dwindling resources [Gray and Diamond, 1994].

Within institutions there is demand for evaluative information that is broader in scope and more in-depth than that provided by past evaluations. These demands include providing information for student, administrator, and instructor decision making (Marincovich, 1999); informing the improvement of instruction (Braskamp and Ory, 1994; Kumaravadivelu, 1995); providing legally defensible evaluation decisions (Centra, 1993); supporting unit priorities, including the improvement of overall instruction in the department (Stake and Cisneros-Cohernour, Chapter Five, this volume) and the conduct of effective evaluations with limited resources (Richlin and Manning, 1995); and providing fair portrayals of the increasing complexity of faculty work (Braskamp and Ory, 1994; Gray and Diamond, 1994).

Implications. Meeting multiple demands is a challenge to the success of teaching evaluation systems. The evaluation of teaching usually includes multiple stakeholders with a variety of information needs. One way to help address these needs is to use multiple evaluation methods, each addressing one or more of the demands placed on evaluation. Some teaching evaluation methods and examples of possible needs that each may meet are provided in Table 9.1.

Two of the most pressing demands on teaching evaluations are the need for information to aid administrator decision making (accountability purposes) and the need for information to help instructors improve their teaching (development purposes). In the former, faculty focus on emphasizing their strengths and accomplishments; in the latter, they focus on identifying and understanding problem areas and discovering ways to improve in these areas. Because of the tension that is often created by trying to address both of these needs using the same evaluation data (Morehead and Shedd, 1997), it may be necessary to employ two separate evaluation systems (Cavanagh, 1996; Centra, 1993; Keig and Waggoner, 1995; Peters, 1994). This allows faculty the freedom to focus on improvement needs using development-focused evaluations without having to use data from these evaluations simultaneously to meet accountability demands.

Although using different evaluation methods and systems is desirable in meeting multiple demands, these approaches must often be tempered by feasibility considerations. Resource constraints may limit the number of evaluation options that can be employed. Therefore, another important aspect of meeting multiple demands is setting priorities for the most important information needs so that evaluations can best address these needs. For example, administrative decision making is more pertinent to some evaluations than to others, only evaluations in certain situations need to stand up to legal scrutiny, and not all evaluations need a strong faculty development component. It is important that those who design and plan evaluations consider evaluation priorities and how these priorities may vary in different situations. Neither faculty nor their departments or institutions can afford to expend evaluation resources on efforts that are misguided and of little use to those involved.

Need for Better Use of Evaluation in Faculty Development. Although many teaching evaluation systems were originally developed to help faculty members improve their teaching, the recent push for accountability in higher education has often altered this purpose (Ryan and Johnson, 2000; Weimer, 1990). Increasingly, the primary role of evaluation is to make accountability decisions regarding higher education personnel, courses, units, and institutions. In response to this trend, teaching evaluation and development scholars have argued for greater emphasis on instructional improvement in the evaluation of teaching. For example, Braskamp and Ory

Table 9.1. Teaching Evaluation Methods and Examples of Needs They May Meet

Method	Demand
Student ratings	Understand students' learning experiences and perspectives on the course
Self-evaluations	Promote faculty development
Portfolios	Capture the complexities of teaching
Instructor and student interviews	Understand thoughts, feelings, and experiences of those involved in the teaching-learning process
Alumni and employer surveys	Determine the utility of learning experiences to students' careers
Peer review	Assess instructor knowledge and the value of instruction in relation to a specific discipline; opportunity to gain insights from and share expertise with other instructors

(1994) describe a collegial, supportive approach to evaluating teaching that emphasizes "sitting beside" colleagues in the evaluation process. They characterize this approach as one that includes "team learning, working together, discussing, reflecting, helping, building, collaborating" (p. 13). Similarly, Centra (1993) argues for evaluation efforts that address both formative (improvement) and summative (accountability) evaluation needs. He describes a model for formative evaluation that identifies four conditions that are most likely to lead to instructional improvement: the instructor gains new knowledge from the evaluation, the instructor values this new knowledge, the instructor understands how to change, and the instructor is motivated to change.

Weimer (1990) emphasizes the critical role of formative evaluation in improving college teaching. In her five-step model for improvement, two steps (gathering information and assessing the alternatives) focus on formative evaluation of teaching. Hutchings (1996) has a similar view. She sees teaching improvement as an ongoing, reflective process in which teachers inquire into their own practice, pose questions, and explore alternatives in the company of peers who can offer critique and support. Brinko (1993) emphasizes formative evaluation feedback in teaching improvement. She asserts, "Among all instructional development efforts, the most promising way of fundamentally changing postsecondary teaching is to provide faculty with individualized formative feedback. In this process, information about an instructor's teaching is collected, summarized, and fed back to the faculty member" (p. 574).

Implications. Although many would agree that teaching evaluations should be used for instructional and faculty development, the use of evaluations for this purpose is often limited (Braskamp and Ory, 1994; Weimer, 1990), for a number of reasons. First, to fully employ evaluation as a tool for faculty and instructional development, some current conceptions of evaluation will need to change. Although evaluation as "sitting beside" (Braskamp and Ory, 1994) is appealing, it is unlikely that many people hold this view of what evaluation is or can be. The integration of instructor inquiry, reflection, and exploration in an environment of collegiality, support, discussion, and team learning is a new idea that counters long-held perceptions and experiences. If this approach is to be accepted, conceptions of the evaluation of teaching must be broadened. More evaluators and educators need to learn how evaluation can better serve faculty development needs, and more instructors need to learn how evaluation can help them improve their teaching. All involved need to conceptualize and implement evaluations that emphasize instructional improvement through strategies such as reflection, collaboration, dialogue, and continued inquiry and learning about teaching.

Second, there continues to be tension between the development and accountability purposes of evaluation (Bernstein, 1996; Peters, 1994). This tension, which often leads to an emphasis on accountability at the expense of development (Weimer, 1990), contributes to the limited use of evaluation for development purposes. To ease this strain, approaches are needed in which evaluation for development purposes can be integrated with or exist alongside accountability evaluations (such as evaluations for promotion and tenure). In some cases, it may be possible to provide development and accountability information using the same data as long as the need for one or both of these types of information is minimal. On the other hand, providing in-depth information for both development and accountability purposes using the same data collection procedures may be more challenging than many have been willing to admit. It will certainly be difficult to have one evaluation procedure that meets the need for legally defensible personnel decisions (Centra, 1993) and the needs for instructor self-understanding (Braskamp, Chapter Three, this volume), individualized feedback (Brinko, 1993), and understanding the intentions and beliefs behind instructors' actions (Pratt, 1997). Intense accountability demands and in-depth faculty development needs call for different evaluation methods and procedures. As increasing demands are placed on evaluation for both development and accountability, there is a greater need to separate evaluation activities that address these different purposes.

A Comprehensive Evaluation Approach

Based on issues in the evaluation of teaching and the implications we have drawn from them, we now provide a brief description of initial efforts to develop a comprehensive approach to the evaluation of teaching. The evaluation approach we propose has four components: identification of teaching goals, preliminary assessment of teaching using performance indicators, evaluation to promote continued growth, and evaluation to reach minimum standards (see Figure 9.1.)

Figure 9.1. Components of a Comprehensive Evaluation Approach

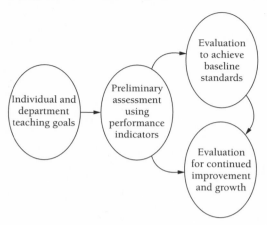

Identification of Teaching Goals. An important component of a comprehensive evaluation approach is an ongoing collaborative effort among department faculty to identify teaching goals. The development of these goals includes dialogue about what it means to be a good teacher in the department and the roles of department faculty in relation to teaching and instructional improvement. This dialogue may also draw on institutional and college mission statements, perspectives from students, and the literature on teaching. As faculty in a department work together to identify teaching goals, they establish a foundation for a learning community (Richlin and Manning, 1995) or a community of practice (Stake and Cisneros-Cohernour, Chapter Five, this volume) in which there is shared understanding and ongoing dialogue about teaching. This collaboration also helps contextualize teaching goals and maximize the utility of the evaluation for the primary users of evaluation results: faculty and administrators in a department. It increases appropriate use of evaluation results by promoting local ownership and understanding of the evaluation process. Collaboration also provides an opportunity for instructors and departments to set priorities for evaluation and development efforts.

Preliminary Assessment of Teaching Using Performance Indicators. A second component of the evaluation approach is the use of performance indicators (Borden and Bottrill, 1994; Wholey, Abramson, and Bellavita, 1986) to assess teaching. Performance indicators are preliminary assessments that provide pointers to the type of further evaluation that is needed. They provide general information on teaching without using extensive resources. For example, performance indicators may include peer review of course syllabi (Chism, 1999) focusing on two or three key areas of instruction such as course content and learning activities. (See the chapter appendix for an example of a form for peer review of course syllabi.) Performance indicators may also include global student ratings of instruction (for example, "Rate the instructor's overall teaching effectiveness" and "Rate the overall quality of this course"). Performance indicators are established through continuing department dialogue that builds on the collaborative efforts to identify teaching goals. Once data from these general indicators are obtained, decisions can be made regarding the type and extent of further evaluation activities.

Evaluation to Promote Continued Growth. Depending on the outcome of initial evaluation results using the performance indicators, faculty participate in one of the two remaining components of the evaluation system: evaluation to promote continued growth or evaluation to reach minimum standards. For example, if an instructor's teaching is deemed satisfactory using the performance indicators, he or she would participate in evaluation activities that emphasize personal and professional development in a community of practice. These evaluations would include dialogue, peer involvement, self-reflection, and a search for better understanding of teaching and its evaluation. The evaluations would be strictly formative, allowing instructors to seek self-understanding, individual goals, and feedback on teaching weaknesses without fear that this information would be used for accountability purposes.

Evaluation to Reach Minimum Standards. In cases where performance indicators flag a faculty member's teaching as below department standards, further evaluation activities would be conducted (for example, using student focus groups or peer observation) to help determine and clarify the specific areas in which the instructor needs to improve. Instructional development specialists would provide additional insights and direction. Appropriate development efforts would focus on specific areas of need, and benchmarks for improvement would be established. Departments and institutions would make every reasonable effort to help instructors improve their teaching in the specified areas. This process makes it clear to instructors the changes they need to make and provides resources to help them improve in these areas. Once performance consistently meets department standards, the faculty member would be free to focus on evaluation for continued growth. In cases where improvement does not occur, the documentation of this process provides a defensible basis for actions that the department or institution may take in response to continued poor instruction (for example, not granting tenure or promotion).

Conclusion

A substantial body of literature on the evaluation of teaching has contributed a great deal to our understanding of teaching and its evaluation, but there are still fundamental areas to address. There is need for evaluations that are based on clearly identified faculty roles and expectations and an understanding of specific teachers and teaching contexts. Evaluations of teaching must address multiple demands that are placed on them. They should also provide better information for and be better integrated with faculty development efforts.

In an effort to address these needs, we have sought to describe a comprehensive approach to the evaluation of teaching. This approach includes initial work in identifying individual and department teaching goals. Based on these goals, teaching performance indicators are developed and used to determine the type of continued evaluation activities in which instructors will participate. This approach makes it possible for efforts to be tailored to individual needs and specific evaluation demands. It also aids in the efficient use of resources in the evaluation and improvement of teaching.

Appendix A: Course Syllabus Peer Review Form

Course: _____ Section: _____ Semester: _____
Instructor whose syllabus you are reviewing: _____
Please rate this course in the following three areas:
1. Course content   ___ Excellent
                         ___ Satisfactory
                         ___ Needs improvement
                         ___ Syllabus does not contain sufficient information
                               to rate this area
   Explain your reason(s) for giving this rating including reference to department goals in this area.

   _____
   _____
   _____

2. Learning activities/   ___ Excellent
   processes   ___ Satisfactory
                         ___ Needs improvement
                         ___ Syllabus does not contain sufficient information
                               to rate this area
   Explain your reason(s) for giving this rating including reference to department goals in this area.

   _____
   _____
   _____

3. Testing and grading   ___ Excellent
                         ___ Satisfactory
                         ___ Needs improvement
                         ___ Syllabus does not contain sufficient information
                               to rate this area
   Explain your reason(s) for giving this rating including reference to department goals in this area.

   _____
   _____
   _____

References

Angelo, T. A. "Relating Exemplary Teaching to Student Learning." In M. D. Svinicki and R. J. Menges (eds.), *Honoring Exemplary Teaching*. New Directions for Teaching and Learning, no. 65, San Francisco: Jossey-Bass, 1996.

Bernstein, D. J. "A Departmental System for Balancing the Development and Evaluation of College Teaching: A Commentary on Cavanagh." *Innovative Higher Education*, 1996, *20*(4), 241–247.

Boggs, G. R. "What the Learning Paradigm Means for Faculty." *AAHE Bulletin*, 1999, *51*(5), 3–5.

Borden, V.M.H., and Bottrill, K. V. "Performance Indicators: History, Definitions, and Methods." In V.M.H. Borden and T. W. Banta (eds.), *Using Performance Indicators to Guide Strategic Decision Making*. New Directions for Institutional Research, 82. San Francisco: Jossey-Bass, 1994.

Braskamp, L. A., and Ory, J. C. *Assessing Faculty Work: Enhancing Individual and Institutional Performance*. San Francisco: Jossey-Bass, 1994.

Brinko, K. T. "The Practice of Giving Feedback to Improve Teaching." *Journal of Higher Education*, 1993, *64*(5), 574–593.

Cambridge, B. L. "The Paradigm Shifts: Examining Quality of Teaching Through Assessment of Student Learning." *Innovative Higher Education*, 1996, *20*, 287–297.

Cashin, W. E. *Developing an Effective Faculty Evaluation System*. Manhattan: Kansas State University, Center for Faculty Evaluation and Development, 1996.

Cavanagh, R. R. "Formative and Summative Evaluation in the Faculty Peer Review of Teaching." *Innovative Higher Education*, 1996, *20*, 235–240.

Centra, J. A. *Reflective Faculty Evaluation: Enhancing Teaching and Determining Faculty Effectiveness*. San Francisco: Jossey-Bass, 1993.

Chism, N. *Peer Review of Teaching: A Sourcebook*. Bolton, Mass.: Anker, 1999.

Cousins, J. B., and Earl, L. M. "The Case for Participatory Evaluation: Theory, Research, Practice." In J. B. Cousins and L. M. Earl (eds.), *Participatory Evaluation in Higher Education*. Bristol, Pa.: Falmer, 1995.

Ellett, C. D., and others. "Assessing Enhancement of Learning, Personal Learning Environment, and Student Efficacy: Alternatives to Traditional Faculty Evaluation in Higher Education." *Journal of Personnel Evaluation in Education*, 1997, *11*, 167–192.

Gitlin, A., and Goldstein, S. "A Dialogical Approach to Understanding: Horizontal Evaluation." *Educational Theory*, 1987, *37*(1), 17–27.

Gray, P. J., Adam, B. E., Froh, R. C., and Yonai, B. A. "Assigning and Assessing Faculty Work." In M. K. Kinnick (ed.), *Providing Useful Information for Deans and Department Chairs*. New Directions for Institutional Research, no. 84. San Francisco: Jossey-Bass, 1994.

Gray, P. J., and Diamond, R. M. "Defining Faculty Work." In M. K. Kinnick (ed.), *Providing Useful Information for Deans and Department Chairs*. New Directions for Institutional Research, no. 84. San Francisco: Jossey-Bass, 1994.

Harnish, D., and Wild, L. A. "Mentoring Strategies for Faculty Development." *Studies in Higher Education*, 1994, *19*(2), 191–201.

Higgerson, M. L. "Building a Climate Conducive to Effective Teaching Evaluation." In P. Seldin (ed.), *Changing Practices in Evaluating Teaching: A Practical Guide to Improved Faculty Performance and Promotion/Tenure Decisions*. Bolton, Mass.: Anker, 1999.

Hutchings, P. "The Peer Review of Teaching: Progress, Issues and Prospects." *Innovative Higher Education*, 1996, *20*(4), 221–234.

Kahn, S. "Better Teaching Through Better Evaluation: A Guide for Faculty and Institutions." In D. Wright and J. Lunde (eds.), *To Improve the Academy*. Stillwater, Okla.: New Forums Press, 1993.

Keig, L. W., and Waggoner, M. D. "Peer Review of Teaching: Improving College Instruction Through Formative Assessment." *Journal on Excellence in College Teaching*, 1995, 6(3), 51–83.

Kumaravadivelu, B. "A Multidimensional Model for Peer Evaluation of Teaching Effectiveness." *Journal of Excellence in College Teaching*, 1995, 6(3), 95–113.

Marincovich, M. "Using Student Feedback to Improve Teaching." In P. Seldin (ed.), *Changing Practices in Evaluating Teaching: A Practical Guide to Improved Faculty Performance and Promotion/Tenure Decisions*. Bolton, Mass.: Anker, 1999.

McKeachie, W. J. "Student Ratings of Teaching." In J. England, P. Hutchings, and W. J. McKeachie (eds.), *The Professional Evaluation of Teaching*. New York: American Council of Learned Societies, 1996.

Morehead, J. W., and Shedd, P. J. "Student Interviews: A Vital Role in the Scholarship of Teaching." *Innovative Higher Education*, 1996, 20, 261–269.

Morehead, J. W., and Shedd, P. J. "Utilizing Summative Evaluation Through External Peer Review of Teaching." *Innovative Higher Education*, 1997, 22, 37–44.

Murray, J. P. "The Teaching Portfolio: A Tool for Department Chairpersons to Create a Climate of Teaching Excellence." *Innovative Higher Education*, 1995, 19(3), 163–175.

Neumann, R. "Valuing Quality Teaching Through Recognition of Context Specific Skills." *Australian Universities Review*, 1994, 37(1), 8–13.

Palmer, P. J. *The Courage to Teach: A Guide to Reflection and Renewal*. San Francisco: Jossey-Bass, 1998.

Patton, M. *Utilization-Focused Evaluation: The New Century Text*. (3rd ed.) Thousand Oaks, Calif.: Sage, 1997.

Peters, R. "Some Snarks Are Boojums: Accountability and the End(s) of Higher Education." *Change*, 1994, 26(6), 16–23.

Pratt, D. D. "Reconceptualizing the Evaluation of Teaching in Higher Education." *Higher Education*, 1997, 34, 23–44.

Quinlan, K. M. "Faculty Perspectives on Peer Review." *Thought and Action*, 1995, 11(2), 5–22.

Richlin, L., and Manning, B. "Evaluating College and University Teaching: Principles and Decisions for Designing a Workable System." *Journal of Excellence in College Teaching*, 1995, 6(3), 3–15.

Richlin, L., and Manning, B. "Using Portfolios to Document Teaching Excellence." In M. D. Svinicki and R. J. Menges (eds.), *Honoring Exemplary Teaching*. New Directions for Teaching and Learning, no. 65. San Francisco: Jossey-Bass, 1996.

Ryan, K. E., Geissler, B., and Knell, S. "Progress and Accountability in Family Literacy: Lessons from a Collaborative Approach." *Evaluation and Program Planning*, 1996, 19(3), 263–272.

Ryan, K. E., and Johnson, T. D. "Democratizing Evaluation: Meaning and Methods from Practice." In K. E. Ryan and L. DeStefano (eds.) *Evaluation as a Democratic Process: Promoting Inclusion, Dialogue, and Deliberation*. New Directions in Evaluation. San Francisco: Jossey-Bass, 2000.

Seldin, P. *The Teaching Portfolio: A Practical Guide to Improved Performance and Promotion/Tenure Decisions*. (2nd ed.). Bolton, Mass.: Anker, 1997.

Shulman, L. S. "Teaching as Community Property: Putting an End to Pedagogical Solitude." *Change*, 1993, 25(6), 6–7.

Skinner, M. E., and Welch, F. C. "Peer Coaching for Better Teaching." *College Teaching*, 1996, 44(4), 153–156.

Smith, R. A. "Creating a Culture of Teaching Through the Teaching Portfolio." *Journal of Excellence in College Teaching*, 1995, 6(1), 75–99.

Stake, R. E. "The Evaluation of Teaching on Campus." Unpublished manuscript, University of Illinois at Urbana-Champaign, 1987.

Weimer, M. *Improving College Teaching: Strategies for Developing Instructional Effectiveness*. San Francisco: Jossey-Bass, 1990.

Wholey, J. S., Abramson, M. A., and Bellavita, C. "Managing for High Performance: Roles of Evaluators." In J. S. Wholey, M. A. Abramson, and C. Bellavita (eds.), *Performance and Credibility: Developing Excellence in Public and Nonprofit Organizations* (pp. 1–13). San Francisco: New Lexington Books, 1986.

TRAV D. JOHNSON is faculty development coordinator at the Faculty Center at Brigham Young University.

KATHERINE E. RYAN is associate professor of educational psychology at the University of Illinois at Urbana-Champaign.

INDEX

Back Issue/Subscription Order Form

Copy or detach and send to:
Jossey-Bass Inc., 350 Sansome Street, San Francisco CA 94104-1342

Call or fax toll free!
Phone 888-378-2537 6AM-5PM PST; Fax 800-605-2665

Back issues: Please send me the following issues at $23 each
(Important: please include series initials and issue number, such as TL90)

1. TL _____

_____

_____

$ _____ Total for single issues

$ _____ Shipping charges (for single issues *only;* subscriptions are exempt
from shipping charges): Up to $30, add $5^{50} • $30^{01}–$50, add $6^{50}
$50^{01}–$75, add $8 • $75^{01}–$100, add $10 • $100^{01}–$150, add $12
Over $150, call for shipping charge

Subscriptions Please ❑ start ❑ renew my subscription to *New Directions for
Teaching and Learning* for the year _____ at the following rate:

U.S.:	❑ Individual $58	❑ Institutional $104
Canada:	❑ Individual $83	❑ Institutional $129
All Others:	❑ Individual $88	❑ Institutional $134

NOTE: Subscriptions are quarterly, and are for the calendar year only.
Subscriptions begin with the Spring issue of the year indicated above.

$ _____ Total single issues and subscriptions (Add appropriate sales tax
for your state for single issue orders. No sales tax for U.S. subscriptions.
Canadian residents, add GST for subscriptions and single issues.)

❑ Payment enclosed (U.S. check or money order only)

❑ VISA, MC, AmEx, Discover Card #_____ Exp. date_____

Signature _____ Day phone _____

❑ Bill me (U.S. institutional orders only. Purchase order required)

Purchase order #_____

Federal Tax ID 135593032   GST 89102-8052

Name _____

Address _____

_____

Phone_____ E-mail _____

For more information about Jossey-Bass, visit our Web site at:
www.josseybass.com   **PRIORITY CODE = ND1**